DUNCAN MINSHULL is a freelance audio producer and anthologist, formerly a senior producer at BBC Radio. His previous books include *While Wandering*, *Beneath My Feet* and *Sauntering*. He has written extensively about walking for publications including *The Times*, *Financial Times*, *Daily Telegraph*, *Guardian*, *Condé Nast Traveller* and *Vogue*.

Praise for *Where My Feet Fall*:

The *Independent* Best Bc

'If you think great travel writing is all about moving through places in another person's shoes, then you need this collection of essays from twenty writers about the pleasure of putting one foot in front of another. From bustling walks through Karachi with Kamila Shamsie, to rain-soaked treks in Germany with Jessica J. Lee, every entry comes with its own unique flavour and makes you realise that this most rudimentary form of transport can be one of the most evocative. Editor Duncan Minshull, who pulled the collection together, has written three books about walking, so he knows a thing or two about it'

HELEN COFFEY, *Independent*

'A new collection of essays both sprightly and ruminative … exploring the delights – and the challenges – of the placing of one foot in front of the other … *Where My Feet Fall* features such appropriately sturdy literary names, among them Richard Ford, Kamila Shamsie and Patrick Gale … Reading about walking in *Where My Feet Fall* allows you to inhabit the walker's imagination fully – surely the ultimate in armchair travel'

HEPHZIBAH ANDERSON, *Observer*

'[A] wonderful new anthology about walking and creative thinking'   *Inside A Mountain* podcast, CHARLIE LEE POTTER

'A beautiful book'   *Walk The Pod* podcast, RACHEL WHEELEY

'Another great book by the writer and editor now established as the go-to authority on walking. His latest is a collection of twenty thoughtful essays … twenty strolls around the imaginations of some great writers'

CHRIS PALING, author of *After The Raid*
and *A Very Nice Rejection Letter*

WHERE MY FEET FALL

*Going for a Walk
in Twenty Stories*

Edited by
DUNCAN MINSHULL

**WILLIAM
COLLINS**

William Collins
An imprint of HarperCollins*Publishers*
1 London Bridge Street
London SE1 9GF

WilliamCollinsBooks.com

HarperCollins*Publishers*
Macken House, 39/40 Mayor Street Upper
Dublin 1, D01 C9W8, Ireland

First published in Great Britain in 2022 by William Collins
This William Collins paperback edition published in 2023

1

Copyright © Duncan Minshull 2022

Duncan Minshull asserts the moral right to be identified
as the editor of this work in accordance with the
Copyright, Designs and Patents Act 1988

A catalogue record for this book is
available from the British Library

ISBN 978-0-00-841414-6

Set in Perpetua
Printed and bound in the UK using 100%
renewable electricity at CPI Group (UK) Ltd

MIX
Paper | Supporting
responsible forestry
FSC
www.fsc.org   FSC™ C007454

This book is produced from independently certified FSC™ paper
to ensure responsible forest management.

For more information visit: www.harpercollins.co.uk/green

In memory of my walking mother,
June Minshull, 1931–2021

Contents

Introduction

Before you follow these wonderful wanderers across the pages of *Where My Feet Fall*, a bit of backtracking – first to April 1336. To the day Petrarch the poet climbed the craggy side of Mont Ventoux in southern France, in 'air fine', and had much to say about it – about fellow travellers, about the terrain covered, about getting high and gazing afar. His was an early pedestrian story roundly written. It examined the reasons for going on foot and noted the good things gained. It paved a way.

It would pave a way to the English Romantics (William Coleridge, the Wordsworths), who used prose as well as poetry to describe moving into nature, and sublimely so. Another, William Hazlitt, went walking to consider the act of walking itself, and in a popular essay told us to venture alone because our friends talk a lot and block the views. After them came the Victorians and Edwardians, acute responders to their own pedestrian heydays, who didn't link it only to necessity (poverty) or recreation (affluence). They talked of roaming urban and indeterminate places and were attuned to a mental aspect. Charles Dickens declared he might 'explode and perish' should he not leave the house every dawn, every dusk. Virginia Woolf said likewise on one of her night walks.

And if the backtracking was to end and we look to more recent times? There has always been a need for air and exercise, for the sights and sounds and aromas, for the hours to slow and the world to reveal. But don't our walks have added intent? More and more we move through nature to address environmental concerns, and to 'rightfully roam'. We move through cities to search and to clarify (we're all psychogeographers now), and to happily snub the wheel. We move everywhere to settle the mind or to fire it up; and often, Mr Hazlitt, we move en masse for reasons of communality. Hiking groups grow; pilgrimages endure; protest marches are a common optic and we parade endlessly; file to stadia and shops and so forth. We pave a way together.

Travelogues and memoirs, nature narratives and social histories record these journeys. But I think it is the shorter account, formally shaped or shaggy, that truly catches the trajectory of a walk. Very satisfying when the course of three or four miles unpacks over three or four thousand words. Giving the whys, hows and wherefores of a primary activity; its changes of direction and mood filling the page, its rhythms caught in the rhythms of the lines. Dickens the tireless tramper delivered a second gem: he said something 'always happens whilst walking', and if it happens in the head or on the road ahead then it can be laid down at essay length. Which after a few twists and turns brings me to the aim of *Where My Feet Fall*. I asked twenty writers to tell us about a journey made – simply this. Now to keep track of them all … let's be off!

*   *   *

The writers, hailing from various parts of the world and travelling various parts, were given a choice – remember an old walk or report on a recent adventure. The invitation came at the beginning of the 2020 pandemic with all of its restraints, yet the second option was accepted by a goodly number. That the pandemic fails to overshadow their stories is good too. Did the relief and freedom and joy of setting out offer an alternative world for three hours, maybe three days? Footing it can do this.

So the twenty signed up and went about things, usually as one of two types. There are those who put the activity at the centre of their work – call them walker-writers, in the steps of a Dickens, a Woolf, friendlier than a Hazlitt. And there are those whose feet hadn't crossed any pages until here. Also joining up are the ambulating outliers. Harland Miller says 'I've always hated walking', before recalling an episode, caused by a lack of petrol, that was memorable for him … alright, it was 'worthwhile'. While Richard Ford leads the collection with mixed feelings – he doesn't own the right gear, doesn't like the wrong weather, but is abroad often and happy to boot, you know it.

Ford uses a lovely bright word to depict his fellow footers, a 'cavalcade'. For *Where My Feet Fall* I wanted the cavalcade to cover as many grounds as possible. Walks are had in the UK and in Europe. In North America and Australia. In India, Pakistan and Japan. During the hours of daylight, dusk and night; come rain, shine and snow. And the travels themselves? Well, some people scale the heights (not Mont Ventoux exactly, but A. L. Kennedy tackles a side of Skiddaw in Cumbria), and some get down with nature. Deeply so, into fields and forests, along lakeshores and coastlines. And city pavements invariably beckon, as do places harder to define. Suburban places for one, and the liminal, almost in-betweenish places.

Sometimes these places are so offbeat that a reason – even a quest – is needed to negotiate them. Or be content to 'drift' through them without expectation. It helps Kathleen Rooney's return from the Horseshoe Casino in Hammond, Indiana, to her neighbourhood in Edgewater, Chicago. All is blaring freeways and skewed signage and sinister objects, hardly fun yet rich in the telling of. With equal curiosity and probably more love, Will Self 'roams' an expanse of eastern Kent once more, where flaring chimneys and rusted turrets and gun-metal waters resemble a new Sublime to him. And as for suburbia itself, Pico Iyer has a home in it, at Nara not far from Tokyo. His daily 'amble' notes how the old (the shrine) and the new (the beauty parlour) lie oddly adjacent; and how the rumblings of a dog at the gate attest to the man's 'foreigner' status in this in-betweenish place.

From the peaks to the pavements, then. Tens of thousands of diverse steps, in diverse footwear, enjoyed in the air fine. But don't many of our walks strike a common chord – in terms of physical movement, that is, and as an inner journey becomes integral to the experience. When our minds go walking too.

A figure enters the Mühlenbecker Forest, north of Berlin – 'Rain. So much of it that I cannot see beyond the hood of my coat. It falls in sheets, vertical and sideways, on gusts of racing wind. Rain waving like laundry clipped to a line' – and despite the wicked weather, most senses are sharp. The visual, for sure, and the aural ('crackling' and 'slapping'), and the felt ('packed dampness of clay' underfoot). And though it is not exactly said, one anticipates a stream of scents wafting over this land of pine and vine. Finding such wonders as 'yellow pfifferlinge' on the forest floor means a fair day out is had, a fair seven kilometres traversed. Only, Jessica J. Lee's walk happens as much in her head as it does physically ahead. She considers the history of nearby Schloss Dammsmühle, and remembers being hereabouts in different seasons and different situations. And the lasting rain acts as an omen for what might be a final visit to Mühlenbecker.

On drier ground, on the Camino de Santiago de Compostela, Ingrid Persaud reckons she's a rookie rambler – 'I forgot to prepare. When I tell you I forgot I mean I never even walked round my back yard two three times.' Still, she's an astute watcher of the people she passes (and the people passing her), and despite a weariness after three days' heat, the journey inside burns bright – 'But the weird thing was that gradually my mind completely relaxed. It was empty of thought, focused simply and entirely on the act of walking. Even as the pain increased, my mind remained clear'. But surely she'll make it to St James? On another well-trod trail is Joanna Kavenna, following a section of the Grande Randonnée number 4, out of Grasse in the south of France, and her mind is full of everything except the direction taken – 'all sorts of crazy things'. It's not a case of reaching the end, more about the next evocation and the next reverie. What else will be fired up en route?

I've always liked a certain idea – that when a path invites us forward, stretching straight and easy, we find ourselves going backwards. Time travel on two feet, as the rhythm of our stride stirs all manner of memories and forgotten moments. But this is better put by others. By Agnès Poirier, a *flâneuse* at most stages of her Parisian life (Paris is *the* great pedestrian city, in this editor's opinion); and by Cynan Jones, as he 'steppingstones' across a winter beach in mid-Wales; and by Sally Bayley, reimagining a lunchtime walk down the curvy Maltravers Drive of her childhood in Sussex.

Staying with the idea of time travel – can't it mean accompanying a fellow spirit? Joining the human flow of New York is Sinéad Gleeson – '*Left, right, left, right*, lungfuls of air' – who's alert to everything and aware that the writer Maeve Brennan caught scenes so acutely here in the 1940s–60s. Lungfuls of air will be needed by Tim Parks and partner Eleonora if they are to keep pace with the bootsteps of Captain De Cristoforis, friend of Giuseppe Garibaldi. A record of the captain's last march fuels their own march along the lake lands of Lombardy, northern Italy, where the present day has a habit of butting in. 'Sunhats … sunscreen, sunglasses … sunburn'; and at the pretty towns passed 'everyone has a dog'.

It turns out this isn't only a book of us, the shoed and booted bipeds. These pages bring mention of and meetings with a cavalcade of other beings, familiar and surprising. Meet the late-night sheep, the Galician Blonds, probable foxes, coyotes and bears; also the Tasmanian devil and the Raegowrapper. And to confirm that our world does come closer on foot, Josephine Rowe, immersed in field life at Bar Haven, Newfoundland, is sensitive to the presence of moose, and of 'moose nests'.

And, yes, everyone has a dog … dogs deliver truths on their travels. A few are distant barkings, but Pico Iyer gets growled at because he has the buttery smell of the foreigner wandering around his Nara suburb. Most dogs 'pad' and 'trot' the pavements, are ordered by one Delhi resident into groups – street dogs to approach at your peril, or their opposites, the imported, domesticated, mild-mannered St Bernards and Alaskan malamutes. And in this city, hit hard by the pandemic, Keshava Guha says hello to a husky – 'By the time I reach him he is up on his hind legs, and a second later two paws press tightly against my lower back. For over a year, during the pandemic of 2020, he was the only thing I hugged.'

Writers are to be found with their dogs. Patrick Gale receives a reminder to depart the desk and get out there – 'the relentlessly punctual whippet slides sharp little paws onto my thigh'. Come night-time, Nicholas Shakespeare exercises a golden retriever called Sancho (named after Panza, and a footballer, he once told me) and notices how his quadruped friend fades from sight, reappears again, glimmering like a 'glow-worm'. Darkness does this – whether in the city, or in a Wiltshire lane – it changes what is seen during daylight into shapes and sounds we wouldn't usually imagine; it transforms behaviour too. And elsewhere, another dog leads its owner on a merry dance across east London, repository of some eye-catching rubbish. During a second walk they arrive at the side of a small lake, as 'buried personal mysteries' rise to the surface; such an interlude with Gogo the beagle reminds Irenosen Okojie of an enduring 'restlessness in her feet'.

*   *   *

Getting ready for Ventoux, Petrarch thinks long and hard on company, and deciding forms the best section of his story (he will ask a brother; they will bicker a lot). I can't help but admire the lone roamers ahead – whether tackling Skiddaw, the margins of the Isle of Grain, the hard shoulder of the M11 – but, like the poet, I'll second those who want to walk with others. This is when Richard Ford is keenest. That's why Ingrid Persaud and Agnès Poirier are drawn to the rituals of the pilgrimage and the protest march, and even have their marching songs. Can't you faintly hear them?

Moreover, friendships matter, are bolstered on the course of a walk. Kamila Shamsie concludes this roll call of walking writers by doing it in a city not known for doing it (Karachi folk should seek their local 'walking track'). And strong is the joy of heading for the local beach with a sister and pals in tow. Naturally there are differences between them: only two of the four live locally, two happen to be 'slow walkers' and two are 'fast walkers', but soon the outing offers insights:

> We turn to wait for the other two to catch up so I can tell Zehra she has joined the ranks of the slow walkers. 'No, no,' says Zehra. 'I've been watching you. You slowed down, Juni sped up. And I slowed down and Saman sped up. We've all adjusted for each other.'
>
> We are all delighted by this, as if it proves something about a give and take at the heart of our friendships.

Which after further twists and turns brings me to you, the walker-reader, happy (I hope) in possession of *Where My Feet Fall*. Whether solo or with others, at a peak or on a street, in the light or in the dark, taking a dog or dogless – here's to being encouraged, moved and amused by the footfalls to come. Perhaps in these times we should be walking more than ever. Perhaps we are due a golden walking age. If so, let's be off indeed. Forward … *avanti* … *avanzar* … *zenshin suru*!

Duncan Minshull
February 2022

Walking, A Departure

Richard Ford

For me, preparing for a walk is a pretty simple matter. I don't come from a line of experienced, sporting exerters and was never a very impressive athlete. So about all I'm willing to do to ready myself for a walk is rustle up a pair of not-totally-inappropriate shoes – sneakers, or even deck shoes, though not wingtips or flip-flops. Mostly I attire myself in whatever I happen to have on when the walking mood strikes me – garments attuned more to the weather than the walk; and certainly nothing 'walk specific' – nothing like those ball-smusher Lycra tights serious cyclists wear that make me uneasy about the men who're wearing them. I don't do a lot of *walk anticipating*, in other words. Doing more would make it seem more serious than I am.

I definitely *do* have to decide to walk, however – rather than, say, just ambling out the front door and heading off. At certain times of the year I will walk most days – though certainly not all days and not at all times of the year. Sometimes I walk four miles (mostly less), though never at a fast clip. Nothing's instinctive or habitual to me about walking, other than walking across the room to fetch something I want, or walking the dog – that is, walking towards a specific goal. Walking I do for, you might say, walking's own sake is not quite a duty, yet is something less than a pleasure – more like going to a slightly boring job where I'm the boss. At its best – for me – walking can be akin to taking a medium-length, economy-class train journey, where I can put my nose to the cool window glass and let the world course past me as in a dream.

I tend to walk only at the ends of days, since my earlier hours are generally full of interesting, significant activity I want to do more than I want to walk. I definitely don't need to physically 'warm up' to walk – to stretch or do deep knee-bends (which I *always* do for playing squash). The nearest I come to warming up might be mentally scrimmaging with the inertia which can easily convince me not to walk at all, but instead to read a book or watch something on TV or have a drink. Of course, if I can persuade my wife to walk with me, it's always better. We can talk while we're walking, which takes my mind off what I'm doing. Walking alone, frankly, is always a test of my patience.

I mostly walk the paved streets in our little town, here on the Maine coast, where there are houses and cars and other pedestrians, but also woods where there are occasionally coyotes and bears and sometimes rabid foxes, so that I feel better carrying a stout stick with me to fight these creatures off, which slightly ups any walk's adventure quotient. But even without these incursions, I can just as easily decide against walking – chiefly weather's to blame (too hot, too cold, raining, snowing, too windy, not enough wind). Also, almost any even trivial physical bother will put me off a walk. Really, I don't want there to be *any* impediments I have to think about – such as something unpleasant I have to do afterwards. Or something pleasant.

I suppose I do have to be in the right frame of mind to take a walk. Not that I'm fussy about what that frame of mind is, any more than I'm fussy about what I wear when I walk. I'm not conscious of ever walking with any plan of achievement in mind – a designated distance to span, or a particular route to take, or anything related to timing. Any such thoughts cluttering my head would detract from whatever it is I *get* when I walk. I do notice that sometimes I'll decide to take a walk if I'm in a bad mood – not infrequent for a novelist – since it seems to be the case that I can 'walk myself' out of feeling peevish and return more chipper. That said, I never walk to 'figure things out'. I've tried that. It doesn't work. Conversely, I'll also walk if I feel energetically optimistic, as if I'd be squandering a good mood if I don't do something *with* it. However, electing to walk can also indicate I'm not energetic enough for squash, or simply don't want to go to the market. Yet, if I do abstain from 'my walk' (as

my wife calls it) I'll generally feel fine about it – as if it didn't matter if I walked or didn't. Sometimes (maybe it's an age thing), I actually *don't* walk but mis-remember and think I did, in which case I feel about the same.

I do believe walking's good for me, though I really don't know *how good* or why. Probably walking in the way I do it is equal to not smoking two unfiltered French cigarettes a day – which I wouldn't do anyway. As with all medical data about walking, reports are generally positive as long as you don't hurt yourself. Looked at this way, I admit that walking is an act I choose *instead* of choosing something else – having that drink, for instance, since I do both at about the same hour. Indeed, I'm quite aware that I often take a walk so as to postpone having a drink, holding it out as a reward for when my walk is over.

Oh, I know there are dedicated walkers who have very different philosophies about walking from mine; walkers who read about walking online and in books like this one, who take walking supplements, do directed walking exercises, join clubs, watch walking videos, wear insignias and talk in chat rooms for hours about walking, and who write seriously about rituals and etiquettes and theories of preparedness so as to guide themselves more open-heartedly to the stepping-off point. Kudos to you all, I say. Caps off. I'm simply not of your clan – not all that serious about walking. And yet, as with most things, I'm in step with the larger cavalcade of humanity. So, I'm willing to bet there are world-beating walkers who feel much the way I do about it. And as far as these driven-to-walk walkers are concerned, I like to think that for there to be *a you*, there probably also has to be *a me* somewhere far back in the road, which, after all, we're walking together, aren't we?

Following Others

Tim Parks

Any path you take you are following others. But it's something rather different to follow others and let them decide the path. In the early hours of 23 May 1859 Captain Carlo De Cristoforis led a small party of men across the Ticino from Piedmont into Lombardy and marched north on the eastern bank to surprise and capture the Austrian garrison in Sesto Calende where the river flows out of Lake Maggiore. On 27 May he fell in the battle for San Fermo, four miles west of Como.

These were the Risorgimento Wars to liberate Italy from foreign occupation. In the summer of 2020, my partner, Eleonora, and I took advantage of our liberation from lock-down, to follow De Cristoforis on his last heroic march, west to east across Italy's lake land – Lago Maggiore, Lago di Comabbio, Lago di Varese, Lago di Como. Fifty miles and some pretty rough terrain. They did it in four days, we in three. But we didn't have any battles to fight. Except with the heat. Constantly in the region of thirty-five blazing degrees.

'Sunhats,' Eleonora proposed. 'Sunscreen. Sunglasses.' She reflected: 'Sunburn.'

For anyone living in Milan, these lakes offer easy daytrip destinations. Hikers love the high mountain paths above them offering shimmering visions of the lakes themselves and the great Italian plain to the south. But nobody walks the lower hills in between. When you follow men who did not have recreation in mind, you inevitably find yourself exploring new places. And enter a new relation with the land. From start to finish they saw every slope and forest, river gorge and hill-top tower in terms of military threat and opportunity. There were ambushes and bayonet charges. We had to study the map long and hard, and make intense use of a path-finding app to discover a walkable way across this variously beautiful, strangely neglected landscape.

Arona was the place to start. On the west bank of Lake Maggiore, some six miles from Sesto. It's a rattly hour in a slow train from Milan's Porta Garibaldi Station. And in fact it was the great Giuseppe Garibaldi himself who was leading this campaign. The Piedmontese had allowed the maverick revolutionary to put together an army of volunteers. Meaning those too young, too old or too politically compromised to serve in the regular Piedmontese army, which was fighting further south. Very little was expected of them. After a long day's march in heavy rain, Garibaldi arrived in Arona late afternoon demanding beds and food for 3,500 men. As soon as he felt sure that local traitors had fed this news to the Austrians, he got his men on the road again, in the dark, and struck.

We also arrived late afternoon. Across from the station the lake was postcard blue. Gleaming. A big Ferris wheel allows a high view across the water: hills climbing to mountains; castles, monasteries, *campanili*. Ferry boats traced foamy zigzags among the lakeside communities. In 1859 the Austrians had a warship, the *Radetzky*, on patrol. They had commandeered all the local boats. They had dismantled the bridge over the Ticino at Sesto Calende. They felt safe.

Arona rolls over for the tourists. But it's done in style. There's a porphyry-paved promenade, vine-draped pergolas, café tables everywhere. Away from the lakeside, narrow streets climb into shade, offering swept cobbles, noble façades, fashion items. GIUSEPPE GARIBALDI SLEPT IN THIS HOUSE, says a plaque. He didn't. He didn't sleep at all. We went to bed early in the no-frills Hotel Spagna, which rubs shoulders with a funeral parlour to the left and blood donor's association to the right. Captain De Cristoforis, it seems, had a premonition his death was imminent. We know from long experience that the key to walking in intense heat is to start early.

*   *   *

Eleonora slices a peach for breakfast and we are out at five thirty. There's a hillside of suburban clutter to negotiate. Rural decay and middle-class pretension. The quickest route would be the lakeside road, but it's heavily trafficked. And the soldiers would have been in full view of Austrian patrols. A bin lorry pursues us upward past sagging fences and crimson oleanders, until, high above the lake, we're sucked up into the silence of the woods.

The history is an alibi. To get us on the move. To give us a route, a challenge, a story. What matters now is the walking. These are the best moments of the day, under thick deciduous foliage, tunnelling through ferns and spindly saplings. Not a soul. But cobwebs clinging to your face, a deer ghosting through the trees. We have light packs, we walk with trekking poles. The regular thud of poles on hard earth draws us into step, weaves a powerful intimacy. As among men marching in silence. A 'beautiful march' one of Garibaldi's men observed in his diary. At a bend in the path, the leader himself stopped and ordered his men to be still. It was pitch-black. They thought he had picked up the sound of the enemy. 'The nightingale,' he said. 'Listen.'

'This is the Parco Naturale dei Lagoni di Mercurago,' Eleonora tells me. She is the map reader. 'The big lakes.'

This is comical when you have the huge Lago Maggiore spread out below while the biggest *lago* we come across up here, glimpsed through sagging branches and tall reeds, is a stagnant pond where lilies float in slimy reflections of overhanging twigs. It's 8 a.m. and warming fast.

'Time for the sunglasses.'

Only one bridge crosses the Ticino here. It's built on two levels – trains below, cars above – right where the lake funnels into the river. So we have to leave Garibaldi and De Cristoforis, who stayed in the hills as far as Castelletto, a mile further south, then crept down to the river and embarked their advanced guard on boats that local patriots had hidden from the Austrians. We plunged down tortuous paths and country lanes back to the main road where the OK Café offers lorry drivers cappuccinos and croissants. Ten o'clock. Having foregone the dinner that the good people for Arona were preparing for them, Garibaldi's men marched on empty stomachs. Eleonora wondered what happened to all that food.

'I guess the people celebrated not having to put them up for the night.'

The views from the bridge are spectacular. Hazy glaciers to the north, above white sails becalmed in blue, a greener, more rivery world of scullers and ducks to the south. Then it's just a stone's throw to Sesto, where an obelisk resting on four cannon-balls bears the inscription:

HERE THE BRAVE CAPTAIN DE CRISTOFORIS
DEFIED THE PERILS OF AN UNEQUAL
CONTEST

We followed the river a mile or so to the place where they crossed. The sun is ruthless now. No amount of cream, no technical quality of sweat-wicking shirts or ventilated hats can subdue it. The skin burns. Fingers and toes swell and throb. You must stay on the move, always. Never stop, if not in the shade. An appropriate imperative when following a man like Garibaldi, whose strategy was never to stay still.

There is no shade on the river bank. The water slides southward, strong and solemn between wooded slopes. There is no monument at the point where the men crossed. The fast current scattered them and it took a while to regroup in the rainy night. Later, in Sesto, the townsfolk came out, repossessed their boats, tied them together from bank to bank and brought 3,000 men stumbling across in the dawn.

Sesto Calende is more real than Arona, with hints of activities that do not require French and German tourists. Being mainly men who had fled Lombardy to avoid Austrian military service, Garibaldi's volunteers were warmly welcomed here and lavishly fed. Arguably, it was the awakening of a spirit of patriotism, a yearning for freedom, that was the achievement of this campaign, more than any military significance. Enjoying our new freedom post lockdown, we bought bread, cheese and tomatoes and found a bench in the shade. I took off my shoes and studied a first blister. Then onward, five more miles to Corgeno, on the shores of Lake Comabbio, skirting rugged hills to the north, filling our water bottles in the fountains of every village: Oriano, Oneda, Mercallo, avoiding busy roads.

No one walks from town to town any more. That's the truth. The Italian word *viandante*, like the English word 'wayfarer', has fallen into disuse. 'Someone who goes on paths outside towns, travelling by foot, to reach distant places,' the dictionary explains. And adds: 'No longer current.'

Hikers take their cars to where the roads end and the paths begin. Looking upward to our left, we can see the peaks we've climbed on other trips. Now we're walking through the debris the glaciers brought down from there: steep, oddly contorted hills, concealing pretty villas, abandoned farms, shallow lakes. A rich smell rises off the soil, dry and honeyed. Stone walls are thick with ivies, alive with lizards. Brambles clutch. A donkey brays. Roused by the click of our poles, dogs chase along railings, barking wildly. Everyone has a dog. Everyone senses the need for protection. The wayfarer passes.

Garibaldi left Captain De Cristoforis with 120 men to protect Sesto while he took the main body of troops to Varese. The Austrians arrived from the south with 3,000 men. De Cristoforis was thirty-four, a middle-class intellectual, who had written books on agricultural reform, studied at a military academy in Paris and taught in London. He placed all his men in ambush at the sides of the road we walked along, let an Austrian cavalry party pass, then sprang out and opened fire from behind. The Austrians broke up while De Cristoforis escaped into the hills to rejoin Garibaldi. Convinced the main army was still in Sesto, the Austrians shelled it. Causing the first Italian casualty. A woman crossing the piazza with her shopping.

After wasting an hour lost in a thick wood, we found no shops open in Mercallo. The August siesta is notorious, but a neon sign beside the town hall wished happy birthday to Ida Brusa, who, spared the cannonballs, had reached the grand old age of 102. By evening we had reached the shores of Lake Comabbio and ate freshwater prawn risotto on a terrace that pushes out among the bulrushes, raising our glasses in celebration when the cruel sun at last sank in the west.

'Did they not get blisters in the nineteenth century?' Eleonora asked.

While Garibaldi marched through the night, we were studying our feet in our hotel room.

'They wrapped their toes in rags soaked in tallow.'

'Which is?'

My bluff was called. 'To do with candles?'

She checked with Google. 'Boiled animal fat.'

*   *   *

We made do with blister plasters and had our shoes on again before dawn, heading north now up the east bank of Comabbio, beside carpets of what look like huge yellow lilies. This is fast, easy walking along well-surfaced bike paths, pleasantly tame, but with the bracing spectacle of the Alpine arc up ahead, gleaming in early sunshine.

Climbing north-east, to cross the hills to the Lago di Varese, it's still flowers I remember. Pushing through foxgloves and yellow archangel. Brushing a small butterfly from my lips. There are horses in the fields, hay bales. Everything is bucolic, becalmed. A summery fragrance tenses for the coming heat. The first wasps begin to buzz. Then the woods close in and the path is little more than a steep cascade of rocks, a dry stream where we find a woman on horseback picking her way with infinite care. Garibaldi had only 150 cavalry, too few to make much difference in a battle but useful for reconnaissance. His scouts told him there were 6,000 Austrians in the key town of Como, already moving west towards Varese. It was important to get there first.

We pass Bernate and Bodio Lomnago. Like pretty provincial women, these villages seem unaware how much their treasures would be admired in the metropolis. Seventeenth-century villas await a first renovation. Churches crumble in romantic neglect. But in the narrow lanes the cars are as fast as anywhere. I have to shout to Eleonora to be careful. It's as though she couldn't see the danger. Eating breakfast on the terrace of a surprisingly well-stocked *pasticceria*, the gossipy ladies at the next table are shaking their heads over a young boy overwhelmed in an avalanche on the slopes shimmering above us. His corpse was brought down this morning.

You dive down the hill now, with Lago di Varese luminous below. Your poles tick off the miles. Rhythm is so important.

Steadiness. We hum to keep time. For a while we're hemmed in by tall walls of maize. The air is oven hot. So the oak woods along the lakeside are welcome. At the delightful little harbour of Azzate, you can rest under willows and gape at the view. Before the thousand-foot climb to Varese.

It's a town of 80,000 people now. There were 11,000 then. 'It seemed every single man woman and child came out to greet us,' Garibaldi remembered. Under drenching rain. We arrived drenched in sweat, desperate for shade. And found it under the elegant portico in Piazza Podestà, together with a list of those who died just forty-eight hours after that triumphant arrival. A bronze statue, striding forward, raises the banner of the Cacciatori delle Alpi – Hunters of the Alps – towards angels with open wings on the church façade above.

'Astonishing,' Eleonora reflects, 'to think how readily people went to their deaths, when we've just been hiding in our houses for three months.'

Varese is a gracious blend of stuccoed antiquity and upmarket window dressing. But our story guides our steps to the Parco di Villa Panza at the top of the town – eighteenth-century English landscaping with Mediterranean vegetation – and the splendid Villa Ponti, built in 1858, just in time for Garibaldi to climb to the roof and gaze down the narrow valley to the south-east – the road to Como – whence the Austrians would surely arrive. His men were already throwing up barricades.

*   *   *

Our dawn departure on the third day led us through the battle-field. I can't recommend this walk. Four miles of busy road, flanked to the right by a gorge dank with neglect and to the left by a ribbon of commercial developments hiding impossibly steep mountains behind.

'People must think we're nuts.'

But there is simply no other way out of Varese in this direction. Fortunately it was Sunday. We moved fast downhill. As did the Garibaldini when they chased the fleeing Austrians. Having waited under fire until the enemy was just fifty yards away, they unleashed a volley of lead, then leapt forward with their bayonets. General Urban had not expected such discipline from volunteers.

The thought of this drama – the bells of the town rang deaf-eningly throughout the battle – put a spring in our anxious steps where the pavement ended and heavy vehicles swept by like cannonballs. At each outlying village down the steep slope – Belforte, Molinazzo – the Austrians tried to take a stand. We hurried past. Until at last a flight of steps to the left – hundreds and hundreds of stone steps through dense foliage – led us up, up and up, to the village of Malnate perched above the gorge. Just ten miles from San Fermo. And the battle.

A wonderful momentum develops now – the reward for this kind of walk – as if the whole landscape were drawing us to the bloody showdown. Everywhere there are signs, pointers. Via Enrico Cosenz. He was commanding one of Garibaldi's three regiments. Via Nino Bixio. Commanding another. Piazza Garibaldi.

'I feel like I'm marching through a history book,' Eleonora observes.

'I suppose the difference is we know they made it; they had no idea what would happen.'

'We don't know,' she objects, 'whether *we* are going to make it.'

The path leads through high, pre-alpine meadows. *Sound of Music* country. Flowers and cowbells, and hawks circling above. Waiting for the kill. Garibaldi had sent a small detachment ahead along the main road to Como, below. A bluff. General Urban regrouped to block their way, at Camerlata, where a break in the chain of hills allows easy entry to the lakeside town. Instead the bulk of the volunteers had taken the high paths. There was a narrow pass just beyond San Fermo.

We speeded up to keep pace. Through fields of corn stubble. Past a class of well-to-do folk training their pedigree dogs. Many of Garibaldi's men were well-to-do. More students than peasants. Many had long pedigrees. Lawyers, engineers, artists. 'They didn't march in silent lines, like soldiers,' wrote a witness. 'But cheerfully, in groups of friends. Like a caravan in the desert.'

'For sure, this is desert heat.' Eleonora sighs. Her calves are burning. She laughs at my red nose. For the nth time we cream each other up and toil on. Village after village. Olgiate. Soldo. Cavallasca. Via 27 Maggio tells us we're in the zone. Walking on roads again now. Eager to arrive, relieved we won't have to fight when we do. Ominously, Via San Fermo becomes Via Carlo De Cristoforis, climbing steadily between flowering hedges and stone walls where the soldiers pressed themselves for cover approaching the narrow entrance to the village, church to one side, villas to the other. A garrison of six hundred Austrians ready to fire.

It was supposed to be a simultaneous three-pronged attack.
De Cristoforis was riding an old nag he had bought in Sesto.
His excitement betrayed him. Someone fired a shot and
he ordered the charge a moment too soon. Carved from
the rocky hillside exactly where he fell, his memorial is all
but overgrown with dry ivies, lavender, spiky yuccas. Still
under fire, Garibaldi kissed his dying captain on the mouth and
hurried on.

'On the mouth?'

'So a witness said.'

Fortunately a plane tree offers shade in the piazza beyond the
church. It's a surprisingly generous, wide open space, with jets
of water spurting from the stone paving in teasing rhythms.
A little girl times tricycle attacks between the nozzles when
the jets fall. There are cypresses and pink oleanders. We eat
our sandwiches on a stone bench, studying the inevitable
monument. Fourteen Italians died. Sixty-eight Austrians.
Hundreds wounded.

'I suppose everything comes at a price.'

'Even a walk.' Eleonora peels off her socks to put sore feet in
the water of the fountain.

And still the day isn't over. With General Urban witlessly
defending the main road, just south of Como, Garibaldi at once
descended the tortuous Valfresca that twists and turns in a
precipitous thousand-foot plunge to meet the lake just to the
west of the town. You need to tread carefully here as you seem
to burrow right down into the heart of the hills, through tangled
vegetation thrusting from dusty cliffs, with the constant sound
of water trickling in hidden crevices. Until all at once – and it
startled us – you turn a corner and gloomy canyon flings open
into fabulous panorama: mountains all around soaring straight

from the blue dazzle of the lake, villas and castles clinging to their sides, and the pretty town of Como just below, waiting for its heroes with open arms. And Eleonora breathes ... 'Italy to die for.'

We Going Santiago

Ingrid Persaud

My birthday catch me in Sarria – a small town in Galicia, Spain. Well, 'catch me' is not exactly correct. I'd flown from Barbados and was about 112 km of steep, hilly ground from where I wanted to be: Santiago de Compostela. Reach the cathedral there by my own two foot – allegedly where St James the Great is buried – and I would have officially walked the famous Camino de Santiago de Compostela.

Two other Trinidadians, dear friends Christopher and Jacqueline, and a Barbadian (we call them Bajan) made up the posse, and we gave ourselves a cool six days to cover the distance. I had a small disadvantage compared to the others: I forgot to prepare. When I tell you I forgot, I mean I never even walked round my back yard two, three times. I didn't pack properly. Inside my suitcase was a pair of cheap, spongy shoes only slightly better than flip-flops, no socks, a set of white and black T-shirts and linen shorts. Rather than being ready to tackle the hot, dusty trek ahead, I had clothes for a weekend lime. This was a case of extreme inverted snobbery. I hate people who can't stretch their legs without specialist, fancy gear. My response? Show up physically, materially, emotionally and spiritually unprepared. I am willing to bet not a single *peregrino* (pilgrim) I met along the way was in such a poor state.

Day one of the camino (literally 'the way') started with a steep climb through lush green vegetation that went on and on for several kilometres. Guidebooks described this segment as 'challenging'. Yeah, right. 'Challenging' was another way of saying you will feel like you're going to dead. My shin hurt. My back hurt. But of course everybody was doing their own unique camino. I was there dying while Christopher and Jacqueline were busy scampering up like two mountain goats.

It was on this first steep uphill that I remembered a friend, Corrie, had sent a message encouraging me to use walking poles. The Bajan had some he wasn't using, which I borrowed and 'forgot' to return. Christopher and Jacqueline whizzed past on that first incline and finished several hours earlier, while the Bajan kept me company. And that became the daily pattern. Of course they weren't the only ones to pass us. There was a set of young people strolling like they were cruising around town. A delicate Japanese woman, with a backpack weighing more than she, moved *voosh*. Old-timers. A lady carrying a baby on her shoulders. I managed to keep up with a lovely, middle-aged Italian called Gabrielle, but only because her knee wasn't working too good.

We had started around 8.30 a.m., and with few breaks it took me until 3.30 p.m. to complete the 23 km to Portomarín, our first overnight stop. In those last three hours of walking I thought the blistering sun would kill me and I slowed to a crawl on the melting tarmac. As if reaching Portomarín wasn't nuff, there was yet another steep hill between me and my bed for the night. Halfway up that last so-and-so incline I collapsed at the side of the main road and cried like a baby. The Bajan had no sympathy. He said everyone had come on this trip because of my birthday, so I had damn well better do it.

I would tell you to pull your socks up, except of course you brought no socks, crazy woman.

Somehow I hobbled up the remainder of the hill to the room, where I lowered myself into an ice-cold bath followed by a bottle of peppermint oil on my mashed-up foot. Then it was straight into bed without bothering to eat. This became my daily, post-walk ritual. Somewhere in my drowsy state I heard the Bajan ask if I wanted to join the posse for dinner. Too tired to even open my jaw, I muttered something about being exhausted beyond belief. Was he feeling the same vibe? Hear him:

No, I have reached my limit but not exceeded it.

My last memory is of drifting off to sleep plotting murder. Near midnight, he came back quiet with a container of spaghetti and tomato sauce. He real lucky because that pasta made me postpone any 'accident' I had planned for him.

The second day, with the memory of yesterday's heat, we started an hour earlier. An even steeper incline was waiting, and that was the path for a couple hours. Every time I looked up, I could not imagine reaching the summit. When I did reach what I thought was the summit, would you believe it had a next summit up ahead? I would've sat down and bawled my eyes out again, but for what? We were in the middle of the Galician countryside. Everywhere were hills. The only way to the next town was by walking. So I walked and walked, all the while guzzling water like a camel and sweating like a piggy.

And I had to ask myself, since I don't have religion, why was I making this pilgrimage at all? I had plenty time to reflect on a life of borrowing from everybody else's rituals to nourish my own spirituality. When Diwali reach, I light dyas. I love Christmas carol services. Come the end of Ramadan I will be wishing Muslim friends Eid Mubarak while sharing their feast. And here was the way of St James, a way to walk one's faith or for me a physical path for reflection.

Another eight-hour walking day was followed, as before, by collapse into an ice bath, anointment of feet with peppermint oil and one hard sleep. All my body begged for was regular topping up with water, a handful of almonds, a few cherries in season and plenty ibuprofen. God bless Pfizer.

The Bajan could easily have walked faster, but to his credit he lagged behind with this slowcoach every day. Now I like walking in silence. He is a talker. His first attempt at ol' talk was about the beautiful wildflowers around us like the wild roses, lilacs and cowslips, and the blistering heat. From there he leapt to a book he was reading about British slave ownership. Researchers were now exposing those who received compensation when slavery was abolished. Fascinating, important stuff – but when all my brain could process was putting one foot in front the other, he was talking to himself. He gave up. The next day, before he could try a next conversation, I suggested we sing. No one was around so we began belting out 'Amazing Grace'. We'd just done the first verse when the Bajan cut me off to explain the history of how that song was written by a slave trader turned holy man. What to do? I let the man talk and talk and talk.

Now Christopher in our posse is a big-time lawyer, but in his heart, the man's a calypsonian. Come carnival, he's on stage at his firm's annual calypso competition singing about whatever chaos and commess going on in Trinidad. Of course, a camino with a calypsonian would be incomplete without a special song for the road. To the tune of Calypso Rose's 'Ah Going Down San Fernando' you should hear him belting out:

> We walking the Camino
> We going Santiago
> Trinis and Bajans, we going sweet
> We wish Buen Camino
> to pilgrims in de street
> Come leh we go
> Santiago.

Now how many people can boast about their own theme song for the camino? Coupled with their kindness and jokes en route, I was real lucky to have him and Jacqueline walking the way with me.

Most the time I managed to keep an even pace, but if I stopped, it was then trouble start. My leg muscles would seize up. Once the daily trek was over I could only manage what my pal Elena calls the 'Chikungunya Walk' – hobbling like I real old, arthritic lady. Even now the memory of it causes me to wobble little bit.

It wasn't all pain. One of the best things about the camino was the sense of community. As you pass one another, no matter if you're ready to drop down, you must greet fellow peregrinos with 'Buen Camino'. Nice and simple, and depending on your tone, it could mean 'good morning', or be a way of showing you understand the pressure they're under. Even the animals were busy greeting us. Enter a hamlet and it's one set of cocka-doodling from the roosters, and more than once we had to make room for herds of massive Galician Blond cows, sauntering to and from pastures coloured by yellow, purple and pink wildflowers.

The people that you meet on the camino you often bounce up over and over. Other times you only meet someone for a few fleeting minutes, but they make a lasting impact. Fifty-something Tiffany from Wisconsin was outside America for the first time. She gave me a top tip about using the walking poles more effectively, then scampered ahead never to be seen again. With each uphill stride I silently thanked that lady. Phil from Arizona spent the last couple hours of one long day walking with us and shooting the breeze. That man could also talk. He talked so much I hardly noticed a good 10 km melt away. Another day we met a fella in charge of seventy young people, aged seventeen to nineteen, doing the camino. If the Pope's looking for sainthood nominations, put down this man's name right now.

A super-fit Australian couple we met early on became confused and I think a little vexed when a slowcoach like me appeared to be getting ahead of them. First day this happened they stayed quiet. Second day they still didn't say boo. Third day they had had enough and stopped me to find out how exactly a snail was ahead of them lean, keen gazelles. Poor things – they thought this was a race. I explained I was getting up early early while it was still making dark to avoid walking beyond 2 p.m. in the heat and dust. They marched off, happy as pappy.

Everyone had their own secret way of getting through the long hours of walking. A group passed me keeping time with a continuous chorus of 1–2–3 1–2–3 1–2–3. A nun recited prayers as she went. I tried to stick close to hear her hypnotic chanting. And gradually the walking became more manageable. My mom emailed a top tip: keep your head down and concentrate on each step. One time I forgot that rule and glanced up at the incline. I shame, but a loud 'oh fuck' escaped my lips and caused the poor nun to watch me cut eye.

One lady called Katie has a special place in my camino. Plenty Lycra-clad walkers hurtle through the camino without fear or doubt. They know they're finishing easy, and, judging by the pace, some were using this as a warm up for the ultra-endurance Marathon des Sables. Katie is seriously overweight and was bowed by a big, heavy backpack. Like me, she was always hot. Her solution? Walk in the mornings and as soon as the midday sun hit, you go inside and rest yourself. She was tackling the full length of what is known as the 'French route', over 780 km, with slow, quiet determination. Whatever her reason for walking the camino I have no doubt she reached Santiago, and would not be surprised if she then continued to Finisterre, the end of the earth.

The thing with pace is you go faster to reach somewhere quickly. But what if, despite the pain, heat and dust, you don't want the moment to end? Yes, my whole body was paining me. Yes, I was exhausted. But the weird thing was that gradually my mind completely relaxed. It was empty of thought – focused simply and entirely on the act of walking. Even as the pain increased my mind remained clear. Years now I've been failing at mindfulness, of being in the moment, and suddenly I was practising it while my aching limbs protested at having to carry me yet another kilometre.

I also found I'd developed a heightened awareness of my surroundings. Galician countryside is full of *hórreos* (grain stores) and *cruceiros* (stone crosses) that can be quite fancy. I was real happy in the shade of the old oak forests with the added magic of wind rustling through the leaves in surround sound stereo. Over the fourth and fifth days we walked inhaling the overpowering scent of the eucalyptus trees. Imagine living inside a comforting tub of Vicks VapoRub and you'll get the vibe. Who knew that the way to complete mental relaxation involved trampling through Galicia with blisters on your two little toes?

On day four I went with my fast self and cut my toenails shorter, hoping to relieve the pressure they were taking on downhill trails. What I didn't expect was the gush of clear liquid followed by watery blood that flowed from under the nail bed. Jacqueline insisted I borrow from her stock of little green socks. I gave in and that saved the toenails from falling off on the walk.

To qualify for the compostela issued by the cathedral in Santiago, places along the route must stamp your *peregrino*'s passport at least twice daily. Every little bar, church and B&B had a unique stamp. A former Paralympian with a T-shirt stall had the fanciest one, sealed in vermillion wax. But the most welcome stamp was in the middle of the forest next to an unmanned fruit stall. Tucked at the side of the stall was a small sign asking a one euro contribution for each box of fruit taken. I lick down some cold watermelon and cherries from that stall and hands down they were the sweetest ever.

A few people have asked if I ever got lost and the truth is not often. As we started walking earlier and earlier, often outside was pitch-dark. Them times a weak moon might help, or maybe a fellow *peregrino*'s faint torch. Once, in the middle of a dark forest, we had to wait until someone came along to literally light the way. By daylight it's easy to follow the yellow arrows and concrete markers counting down the distance to Santiago de Compostela. Plenty times we had the path to ourselves. This was especially true on the last few days when we walked through shaded glades. Without the hot sun I barely noticed covering the 17 km of walking meditation.

By this stage I was coping well enough to eat dinner with the posse. Usually our evening meal was in a rustic B&B we had booked in advance. Apart from one hostel that felt like a jail, most were charming places with good home cooking. Casa Brandariz in Arzúa came with its own chapel and Carmen, a talented cook. At O Muiño de Pena, in Rúa O'pino, the salad and vegetables were picked from the garden a couple hours before dinner. The manager also personally laundered my only black shorts, which I wore daily.

Inevitably, by heaving one aching foot in front the other, the day came when we reached Santiago de Compostela. I expected

to immediately see the cathedral that marked the official end of the walk, and to glide forwards on a red carpet with majestic bagpipes playing. Instead the route meandered on and on through the suburbs with few yellow arrows showing the way. Even within the centre it wasn't straightforward finding the cathedral. When we did, it was at the same time as several other *peregrinos* we had seen on our journey. The Bajan sighed with relief and asked please – could he have his walking poles back? We touched the cathedral walls with grateful hands, and in that moment, I knew *why* I had walked. And since I am borrowing from other people's religion it is not surprising that on the threshold of one saint's grave, I am reminded of another. St Francis of Assisi's words flood my mind. Life is about giving love rather than seeking to be loved. We are here to console rather than to be consoled; to understand rather than be understood. The camino, my very broken hallelujah, was showing the way …

Skiddaw

A. L. Kennedy

Before I climb Skiddaw, there are some things you need to understand.

In Scotland to walk is to climb. The idea of ambling in meadows can seem both luxurious and really dull – proper walking is uphill. In hilly cities, hilly landscapes, enjoyment and high views are paid for in sweat. I think that's part of why Scots won't find it shocking should you suggest life is hard. We don't have Hollywood endings – we have hills. Our up and downhill country has marked similarities to Calvinism's Swiss birthplace. Perhaps this may have helped us embrace that particular form of Protestantism's heady joylessness and cruelty with such passion – *for every pleasure, you must pay*. Mountain people are potentially nearer to heaven, but also to God's wrath.

I would be foolish to generalise, but perhaps I am able to say that access to punishing inclines provokes responses which transcend the physical. After all, when we are tired but have to go on, what pushes us? Mind? Will? Spirit? Soul? Our Other Self?

That 'Third Man' ghost companion is regularly described as appearing to explorers *in extremis* who labour on high. As a species we seem to expect we will encounter mysterious entities when we leave the world's usual level of operations, whether we're climbing a cliffside, a palace tower or a ziggurat, or we're inside the tractor beam of the UFO lifting us into strangeness. And we seem to have a longing for elevation. Achieving a peak feels so much better than trundling downhill like a mindless pebble. Any object can descend – living things fight gravity and rise. This may be why so many religions have laid claim to significant peaks with high altars and places of sacrifice. Mankind has built artificial ascents with pyramids, minarets and spires that reach for heaven. The tall shikhara of a Hindu or Jain temple translates as 'mountain peak'. Of course.

Totalitarian movements have a taste for mountainous structures to dominate mass belief. Albert Speer, Hitler's favourite architect, had a gift for producing chilling scale – heights with only shadow and no wonder. The Nazi cult of paranoia and indulged cruelty even appropriated several sacred mountains. Stonework designed to cow us blocks our view of real mountains, yet somehow we remember the help we find up high. *I will lift up mine eyes unto the hills, from whence cometh my help.*

To undertake a climbing journey, to rise, is no small thing. Even if you are not Abraham, taking Isaac for a nervous stroll with a knife and only one water bottle, ascents are never simply a matter of passing from A to B, or of taking exercise. Whatever our belief systems, we regularly think of lifetimes and experiences as journeys. We *go through* events, as if they were terrains with gentler and steeper inclines. And when we climb together, we draw closer, rely on each other more. The 2020 pandemic revealed that new togetherness shared by people forced to navigate a horribly tilting reality. Landscapes help create our metaphorical progressions. The more forceful their effect on our bodies, the deeper the effect on our minds. I sat in lockdown, but read books about hiking, walking, enduring, achieving prodigious journeys. I was immobile, but far more healthy and pain-free than during my last lockdown – ten years of physical isolation and immobility caused by a long-term back injury. One journey in pain had prepared me for another. During both, I promised myself I'd get through and go back to life, do more and be more. That meant I was promising I'd climb.

*   *   *

My climbing began early, in Dundee, a city built around the slopes of an extinct volcano. The first house I can recall was at the bottom of a steep hill in sight of the Tay River. My early explorations panted up narrow, still-cobbled lanes between high Victorian walls – they had names like Strawberry Bank and Step Row. To four-year-old legs the whole place was exhausting. Our next home was halfway up another part of the same anxiously angled hillside. Winters were all about falling: slapstick democracy and sudden harm. For some reason, although we lived in a Nordic climate, Scots in the 1970s seemed unwilling or unable to dress for the weather. Like everyone else, I stumbled about in thin coats, useless hats and dangerously unsuitable shoes. Heading to school before sunrise and after sunset, in my draughty school uniform, I seemed to be always cold and always fighting gravity. At school assemblies we were regularly offered Bible stories about presumably warmer desert mountains and given the consolation of singing the 23rd Psalm. This was clearly a favourite hymn with the administration and yet it always seemed a little alien. Between the ages of four and seventeen I stood and sang at class-appropriate points in the same hall and pondered the idea of being gently led into green pastures. Beyond the fact that I am not a herbivore and cannot survive on a diet of grass, I found the words conjured up a lush, flat green that was nowhere I really knew and nowhere that seemed to belong in the Middle East. Was God going to take me to Surrey? East Anglia?

My three years at university allowed me to be surprised by the Warwickshire countryside. The pastures were green and gentle here, but I missed the challenge in walking and felt anxious, somehow. With no hills to stand in the way, almost anything might surely race in at you, only slowed a little by picturesque spreading oaks and motorway service stations. And how did you really see anything when you could not get up above it and look down?

I moved to Glasgow and different slopes in the slippery winter of 1987. I found it a bigger, more confident place, genuinely a proper, gallus city, but still unmistakably laid over landscape. There were hills trapped under the tarmac and paving and they gave views to distant, rising green: maybe the Campsies, maybe Cathkin Braes, almost certainly Ben Lomond. The whole city is an incitement to get out and ramble. I became a West Ender, sweated up Peel Street and Highburgh Road, dreaded the ice that gathered on Horselethill Road. My driving lessons were filled with hill starts. In the strange winter of 1995 record low temperatures saw the manly men of Glasgow die in their T-shirts and every slope become treacherous. My bare fingers froze to cash machine buttons and Byres Road tottered, everyone dizzy with shallow breathing to save our lungs from ice. Nature seemed finally punishing enough, even for the Scottish mind-set, and shopping became polar exploration, complete with sundogs.

And, of course, I did answer that incitement to ramble. In Glasgow and the West of Scotland hillwalking demonstrates ordinary people's right to roam: the wee bauchle men of dark streets and single ends, gleefully treading the heather where only landowners and their servants were meant to belong. The mass casualties and traumas of the First World War sent Glaswegians to the hills for solace and the habit of walking stuck. I soon learned the friendly names of routes and summits: Ben A'an, The Cobbler, Ben Lomond, the West Highland Way, the Devil's Staircase from Altnafeadh to Kinlochleven, the route to the Drovers Inn – they are a common part of Glaswegian conversation. And soon I was waking early, packing sandwiches and a flask and heading off in crowded cars for expeditions to walk and climb with strangers and friends. At the end of any hike we would be simply friends – the harder the route the faster the affection.

I learned that waterproofs are necessary – and a balaclava, proper gloves, a comfortable backpack. I learned how much water and food I need. I learned my natural pace. I found the point where I feel I am defeated and the point after that, where I am not. Climbing allowed me – a writer, a cerebral creature – to talk with my body for hour after hour, to listen when I usually ignore it.

My holidays became opportunities for walking. I confirmed my pace with a month's trail-climbing in Jordan and Egypt. I scrambled to places of high sacrifice in Petra, plodded up Mount Sinai in the dark to be ready for the sunrise. As I rose, the mountains that turned around me were pictures from my *Children's*

Illustrated Bible, come to slowly spinning life under riotously bright stars. Nuns and camels, tourists and pilgrims, quietly mingled and ascended. Belief and endurance were being expressed in sweat and mountains. In New Zealand on a week's trek I discovered that I am competitive, that I drive on ahead – in part to test myself and in part to be alone with whatever is waiting to happen when I reach it. All around the world, so much always does happen – the startled red deer, the bear foot-prints, the ravens dancing and whirling as they hold each others' feet, the massive sweep of a sea eagle, the wild cyclamen flowering above the Danube, and the full spectrum roar of that sunrise on Mount Sinai as it burned colours into the pale sea of lower mountain tops receding all around to the horizon.

Naturally, you might climb Mount Sinai to reach up and chat with God. Naturally, God might bend low there and hear you. Ancient Rabbis indulged in wordplay and puns using *nissim*, the Hebrew for miracles, *siman*, the word for a good omen, and *Sinai*. And wouldn't good omens and miracles always be up high? Wouldn't Muhammad ascend from a hilltop and Jesus give up his body on a hilltop and wouldn't you build your First Temple on a hilltop and worship Yahweh there, just as others worshipped Asherah and Baal and the Host of Heaven? The fact that all those things allegedly took place on the same disputed hilltop is enough to splinter the world. Mountains have power.

Sinai didn't kill my walking shoes – that was New Zealand and the Abel Tasman Coast Track. I finally bought my first pair of good boots in a Glasgow January sale – Brashers – they lasted twenty years of dubbin and scrambling and plodding in the US, Canada, Ireland, England and Scotland and round and round boat decks crossing the Atlantic. I still miss them.

Over three decades I have gathered the right kit for a day's walking, prioritising my own comfort and sensibilities in ways I often don't elsewhere. The kit does just as well – and gets more use – as a means of maintaining myself on tour. It supports me on delayed trains, in hotel picnics, comforts me in railway stations and in oceanic gales, adds warmth and emergency rations. One cupboard in my study holds water bottles and backpacks for all occasions, foldable cutlery, power bars, compactable down jackets, gloves, collapsible crockery, first-aid kit, thermos, sunscreen, solar charger, miniature speakers, torch – all the odds and ends that keep things pleasant. Writers are always travelling. Or they were until the pandemic. Once again, nature has decided to show us it can always make us fall.

* * *

What turned out to be my last walk in a long while was on 11 March 2020. I was attending a literary festival in Keswick. I had been a participant there before and knew the festival hotel was up above the town and near the base of Skiddaw. I had even tried to fit a climb in between breakfast and my train home on my last visit. I ended up sweaty and foxed, having to give up at Carl Side and come down again. This time I had added in another day to look about, breathe piney air, search for red squirrels, and I brought the gear I'd need to climb Skiddaw in comfort.

As my years spent being a writer have gone by, I have slowly realised that the endless touring involved in my job is only bearable if days are added here and there so that I can stop, walk, climb. Festivals in India, Egypt, Australia and New Zealand involved significant enough travel that even young, busy me would add in time to hike, see the country. I even climbed to see the cliffs and sea stacks at Port Campbell in Victoria – where I was conceived. I was a creature of cliffs from the very start. As the busyness for my career increased, though, the deadlines, expenses and obligations, I began to spend more and more time just getting to venues, working and going home. This was becoming mentally, spiritually and emotionally exhausting as well as pushing me towards physical burnout. I had spent the last twelve months adding pauses, halts, diversions. I would climb the hills of Paris, feel the ghosts of hillsides under my feet, doing nothing but being there and alive. I would be with the smell of turf, or the sight of water, the sound of birdsong – in Germany, Austria, Switzerland, Wales, England, New England and Scotland. Having withdrawn from flat, old London, I moved to Essex and made the best of its salt marshes and big skies. I was coming back to life. Skiddaw was going to be the next step in my plan for rejuvenation – adding in regular mountains.

I know – it took a while to get here, but you have to be ready for a mountain. You have to check who you are and then, when you meet, it will tell you if you're right.

My festival event passed pleasantly and I slept knowing I would be free the morning after, free and walking. Although audiences were depleted by growing unease about the possible spread of infection and some participants were cancelling, the events rolled on. There were dinnertime arguments about whether the pandemic was serious, or even real. Some authors were delayed by train trouble. There is always train trouble. I had arrived a day early for my event – it's always wise – and felt smug about it and my extra time with the ferns and moss and the vaguely mystical gaze of the Herdwick sheep. And, meanwhile, I touched surfaces and talked to people and breathed.

When I woke the following day, the weather was pleasant, not too warm. I ate a good breakfast – as I almost never do unless I'm walking – and set off through Millbeck past the kind of semi-secretive valleyside houses that always make me imagine other lives I might lead and increases in my happiness related to dry-stone walls and whitewash, old gardens, safe continuity of occupation. When I was a child, travelling by train to and from holidays at my grandparents' house, I would look out of windows and see the flicker of walls in meadows, between trees, at lakesides and think – *There, that's where everything would be all right.* It's a habit I have never shaken. Set me down anywhere and I will find the house where I could live a better life. I already knew there were several along my route.

Winds had been forecast at 50 mph, but ambling along between trees I didn't feel it and could continue to ignore what that might mean. Today was, after all, the only day I had to climb, so I was going to, no matter what. I passed above the bizarre bubble of wealth and spa-going which is the Underscar Hotel and headed to Latrigg Car Park, where the climb would really begin for me. Although there were a few people around, I was glad the prospect of winds, or fatal infection, seemed to have kept numbers fairly low. I wouldn't need to race ahead of people to be on my own. I had my power bars, my reservoir backpack, a handy little map downloaded to my phone. This was going to be lovely.

Of course, the straggle of walkers descending the stiff zigzags of Jenkin Hill did look a little – what? – maybe cold, maybe stunned, maybe raddled. I pressed on.

The incline recommenced the usual conversation between walking and halting, climbing and turning, pain and the ending of pain. It's always the same. Do you go on? Do you give up?

Walking is climbing and climbing is a conversation about how much you will stand. After ten years of back pain, I know a little about how much I will stand. I take opportunities wherever I can to show myself that I am well – to endure discomfort by choice. I exercise daily, lift weights, kayak, walk and walk and walk – even on a day in London, I walk up and down stairs and escalators in the Underground and try to imagine I'm picking my way up rising paths – Grande Grève on Sark, Carnan Eoin on Colonsay, all the dear, far places. My body is pain-free now and I am aware that I am fighting to keep it that way, to strengthen and save it. I am also in training to face being old, that close, hard thing.

Of course, on the London Underground there is no weather, only overheated fug and recycled breath and various infections. Around halfway up Jenkin Hill as I climb Skiddaw, the winds are noticeably disruptive. I veer between concerns that I may be pushed off the track by sideways gusts, or worn out by sweating grinds against 50 mph rain. But, the higher I climb and the stronger the winds, the more possible it is, following a favourable tangent, to spread my arms and lean back, letting myself be shoved upwards in fits and starts. It's a bizarre, exhilarating sensation, like the intervention of a minor deity.

By now my face is mostly numb, even inside one layer of cloth, and my nose is permanently running. The route is dotted with potentially infectious paper handkerchiefs, freshly blown from other cold-clumsy hands. My pocket slowly fills with damp white tissues.

And why is it so pleasant to feel that burn in my legs and that slight rawness at the back of my throat from deep breaths of cold air? It's a proof of life. It's a proof of fitness. It's winning the chance to look back and down and see how far I've come. I never get that now, living in flat Essex after flat London – they lack perspective, they lack scale. Never put your parliament in a place that lacks perspective – put it high and higher, make anyone who wants to work there struggle for it.

By the time Jenkin Hill is over, I feel ready to divert and add in a side trip to Little Man. I'm full, no doubt, of body chemicals that are combining to produce a mild sense of triumph. At this point the view would be good if there were not so much low cloud and so many blinding onslaughts of rain. I could be under the impression that I am almost alone in climbing. Hurrying down past me come all the previous occupants of the higher ground. They seem to have passed beyond enjoyment into somewhere grim. As usual, many couples appear divided: one resentful, one dogged or one viciously happy. I wonder briefly how many divorces happen after climbs like this. I remember my father's fondness for hapless routes and irritable backtracking, his hatred of maps, asking directions, or basic preparation and supplies. He made me an adult who loves good equipment and readiness.

After Little Man, it's hard to ignore the way that snow is lying in each area of shade, or the way the rain is sleet now and painful. But I try. I decide, while I'm up here, to make a further excursion to Sale How. I have time, I have daylight, I have waited three years to come back here. I am asserting my determination to pause the perpetual blurry motion and travel slowly, at a human's pace, to make sure I have time to appreciate how lucky I am. I am not in pain, I love my work, I made it to Skiddaw. I have this one day and I am going to make it count.

Of course, the route to Sale How is scoured by the worst of the wind, it lashes up over the saddle like a vile resentment.

Everyone left up here is in retreat. A man passes me with an aggrieved-looking Labrador – 'It's just silly up there.' I press on, though, slither over semi-frozen snow to a gate, open it and apparently let myself into a whole new area of wind. It's hard to stay upright. I don't. I kneel and look back at figures crouching behind the low piles of rocks left as shelters for times such as this.

Alright then, I'll retreat. My aim was Skiddaw and I only have to reach that to have succeeded. There's a narrow track leading over the saddle between the peak that I won't reach and the one I've fixed my mind on. The track would be my shortest route, but even starting on it feels as if I am being invited to fly – both wonderful and impossible. I retrace my steps, past a father and son enjoying the stillness and the long stretch of snow in Skiddaw's shadow. I sit in the lee of the hill, take off my top layer and add another underlayer. I am freezing but soaked with sweat. My hands are unhandy. I am almost at the point where I can't think. This is, of course, dangerous, but also where I always aim to be – the place where my head turns off and I can be peaceful. I think all day, I am paid to think, I plan and plot and indulge 2 a.m. obsessions, I daydream for fun and daydream for money at a pace that gives me migraines – it takes a few thousand feet to even mute that.

I set off, nothing but determined, to force a way through the heather up the flank of the final rise. There is no path here, but also no wind, with the peak there to defend me. It feels familiar, this *heather lowping*, high stepping over wiry bushes and heading up in a calm that lets my cheeks and forehead recover a little.

The summit is the summit – offers snatches of view between clouds, lake light, satisfaction – but the wind as I break cover almost knocks me off my feet. I have to duck down again almost immediately for another pause, a power bar, a reminder that I can't spread my arms and take off, not safely.

This is success for me, always. I make it — whatever *it* is — and almost immediately some onslaught of unease flattens me and makes triumph unsettling. That Calvinism — it settles in your bones like radium.

The path down is worn-to-the-bare-back stones and a slog. My knee begins to twinge as it always does on descents. It takes me back to Sinai and heading down towards St Catherine's Monastery and its little sample planting of — allegedly — the burning bush. It grows in the most raised of raised beds — up above head height — its terminal shoots endless, nipped off by the long-armed devout. I had climbed Sinai by the camel track, but descended by the Steps of Repentance, which maybe referred to their difficulty — there to make visitors like me repent, sweat our evil out, or maybe referred to a punishment for one monk's sin. (What kind of sin can only be expiated not by building a mountain path of 3,750 steps?) I walked down,

knee twinging, through the arch Elijah was said to have built
and then the one supposedly built by Moses. (Reaching everywhere named after Moses seems to involve climbing. He was a
man of mountains, always climbing high to bother God, bringing back messages, punishments, rules.) Pains make shortcuts
through time that way. You forget them when they're gone, but
then they wake again, they stitch through and join one time to
another. I remember the milk and honey rocks of Egypt as I step
from grey Cumbrian sleet down into grey Cumbrian rain. The
damp lights every scent for miles – all the green tangs of leaves,
heather, peat, coal smoke, live wool, slicked rock, mud and turf.
It's like a symphony.

I limp down Jenkin Hill and as the slope eases so does my
knee and here I am again, returning, grubby and tousled and
content. I remember sitting down in the sun, returned and
victorious by the fortress walls of St Catherine's, eating boiled
eggs and bread while I watched a camel eat an apple and seem
just as happy as any animal can.

And as I head along the tarmacked road to the hotel I pass a
man in the faded walking gear of decades ago, well maintained.
He has a kind face, is white-haired and bearded – as the stranger
you meet on the road in a story always should be. He asks
me, 'How was it up there?' I look, then, like someone who
has climbed.

'Good. A bit windy. But good.'

We nod and we smile like people who are very pleased to be
just where we are at just exactly this particular moment. The
smile makes it perfect. Then he passes on his way and I pass on
mine. I walk on.

I don't know what I learned on the walk yet. I'm a slow
learner and these things always take time, but something will

come, something about embracing the moment and being ready to embrace the moment, maybe something about actually enjoying being alive.

Maybe something like that.

Around Deer's Slope

Pico Iyer

It is a brilliant morning in late November, the radiant season in Japan, when the skies are cloudless, knife-sharp, even as we can feel the coming dark. A perfect day for a temple garden, with explosions of reddening maple leaves outlined against the blue. But I'm walking through a suburb of the eighth-century capital of Nara, built to resemble a residential quarter near Los Angeles. Nearly all the houses are Western-style, arranged in a grid, with silver Priuses and late-model Benzes beside them, in trim garages. The streets are all straight – and spotless – and so little movement is ever expected that there are no pavements, and I can stroll along the middle of the road as if on a film set.

Every last detail in Shikanodai (or 'Deer's Slope', as it would be in English) could not look less like the Japan I dreamed of when I left my comfortable job in Manhattan, at twenty-nine, to explore the quiet intensities of a Buddhist temple on the backstreets of Kyoto. There is not a single shrine or meditation-hall in the area, and nothing that's much older than my Japanese stepson or stepdaughter. There are no lantern-lit alleyways, no women in kimonos, no blonde-wood sushi bars or high-tech emporia. The two main drags are actually called 'School Dori' and 'Park Dori', using the English words, as if to convince my mostly elderly, affluent neighbours that they have retired in Disney America.

But I cherish my morning walk – not least because we have no car or bicycle or media here – and after more than a quarter-century of taking the same walk every day I can do it in my sleep. I amble past the single line of shops – bakery, photo salon, four beauty parlours – and across the park, where the ginkgos and maples dazzle in scarlet and gold. Past the house whose plum-blossoms, pink or white, show above its wall in February, and along the silent street where I'll smell the citrusy perfume of gold osmanthus in early October. Past the home with the basketball net outside its entrance, the cartoon board in the mini-park reminding us to pick up after our mutts, past the house where the dog used to bare his teeth and growl at me every morning, unsettled by my butter-reeking foreigner's scent.

Before I arrived in Japan, I was intoxicated by its tradition of wandering poets. They weren't roaming around lakes and hills like William Wordsworth, but proceeding along a rough, pointed path, in the way of Matsuo Basho. His most famous work – *The Narrow Road to the Interior* – could suggest both the remote areas of northern Japan through which he was walking and the inner terrain that the act of walking would awaken. Monks in the Zen tradition are called *unsui* – 'drifting like clouds, flowing like water' – to enforce the sense that they follow the Buddha on his daily path, sometimes quite literally as they walk around each morning with begging bowls, collecting food.

The destination is never the thing. Some temples in Kyoto, twenty miles away, greet me with characters on the ground, as I step in, that mean 'Look Beneath Your Feet'. Everything you need is here, in other words, if only you're wide-awake enough to see it. And a few hours from where I am now, groups of aged Japanese, dressed in white, are walking among the eighty-eight temples of the Shikoku pilgrimage, and then up to the climax at the great temple-filled mountain of Koyasan, pledging to complete the circuit before they die. In central Nara, I still see men swathed in animal skins, carrying conch-shell trumpets – *yamabushi*, or mountain ascetics – muttering chants before a temple, on a walk that will continue until their final step.

But when I read Basho as a boy, I imagined a narrow path between mountain sanctuaries; heavy snow slowing the pace to a trudge; perhaps a boat moored on a lake, and plovers flying overhead as the skies darkened.

What I didn't see in my romantic dreams was a network of look-alike modern houses arranged in a grid with BMWs parked outside them, and front doors only a few feet from the street. I never imagined I'd be living in a two-room closet in a yellow apartment-block that had been named 'Memphis', in honour of the birthplace of the local god Elvis. Pilgrimage, when I was a boy, suggested something ancient, sacred, bucolic; never a wander past a line of concrete suburban homes where the only houses that are traditionally Japanese – with grey-tiled roofs and wooden gates and bonsai plants behind thick walls – are the ones belonging to professional gangsters, which everyone takes pains to walk past swiftly.

After about eleven minutes, I pass the little building where men are stacking newspapers, next to yet another set of vending machines, and the house whose dog, now confined to his kennel, can barely manage a rumble of alarm as he smells me walking past. In front of me is a flight of steps between thick trees, almost hidden, leading down into another world.

For years I used to take this walk as a break, having done five hours at my desk; a small reward, perhaps, for forcing myself to stay sitting through sunshine and mist. But then I began to notice something: walking shook things loose in me. The very act of ambulation sent my thoughts down different tracks. Movement in some ways – since I had no destination and didn't have to notice where I was going – allowed my mind to run off the leash like a dog on a beach. If I was stuck at my desk, walking could unstick me.

So I started to bring walking into the heart of my writing schedule, and wasn't surprised to learn how many writers place it at the centre of their practice, even if in more urban and less nature-haunted ways than Henry David Thoreau. Philip Roth used to say that he walked half a mile for every page he wrote. Even in his seventies, P. G. Wodehouse was maintaining his discipline of five or six miles a day, which did not keep him from producing more than seventy novels, and in fact may well have made that possible. John le Carré, in my mind's eye, was always walking, looking down, along some narrow coastal path above a cliff, on a blustery day, working through the divided loyalties in his head.

And that's the whole point: walking allows you to inhabit your imagination entirely. Quite often, on this walk, I'm not registering anything around me – only the seaside road in Havana, the Malecón, for a piece I'm writing; or some waist-thin alleyway in Old Damascus where I'm setting the next scene in my novel. Daniel Kahneman, the Nobel Prize-winning behavioural economist, points out that there are certain mental activities (calculating large sums) for which we need to be sitting down; but others (thinking outside the envelope, or deciding to begin a story at its end) we can do best while walking, released into wider horizons. Often, on my forty-minute walk, ideas and sentences build to such a climax that, once I'm back in our flat, whole essays tumble out.

As I descend to the lowest of the well-worn rustic steps, I see a rice paddy to the left of me, bristling and green. A wooden house stands above me on a hill, trees lit up with oranges on the slope leading to it. All the buildings in this village are wooden, and are so few that they might be family members gathered around a hearth. When a van noses through, making a delivery, I have to press myself against a wall so it can pass, at the maximum speed of twelve and a half miles per hour.

I walk through this unexpected outline of an older Japan and up a steep street to an old stone gate, not much taller than I am. Within is Susanoo Shrine, nicely sequestered quite a long way from my bright post-war suburb, and first constructed in 1552.

I climb up to throw some coins into a wooden box, bow, clap my hands twice and pull at a worn rope to ring a bell and summon the gods, and I'm faced with a walled interior, lion-dog guardians on both sides and a chattering wilderness within. Exactly the kind of forested thicket that has been bulldozed down to create suburbs like my own.

I thank the Shinto spirits for protecting us all – Susanoo is the bad-boy god of storms – and then turn back, past the wide-drivewayed house where police dogs are being trained, past the trees bright with yuzu, past my friend from the ping-pong club, planting vegetables against the far-off outline of hills, past country music crackling out of a workplace barn.

Thoughts are beginning to gather now, as they didn't when I was stationary. I take my worn white notebook from my pocket and scribble them down. Thirty-eight years of a rambling writer's life have taught me that few thoughts ever return intact.

Up the rustic steps again, I find myself back in the late twentieth century. Japan as a whole strikes me, increasingly, as a very old, spirit-haunted place wearing the most up-to-the-minute global clothing; often it's only a morning walk that jolts me out of the generic suburb and into something closer to the depths.

Since my early twenties I've been making a kind of living by transcribing foreign places, which in my case means walking around faraway cities. I get off the plane in Mashhad, in Rio, or Sana'a, and walk and walk and walk. For as much of my first forty-eight hours in the place as I can, allowing this new and fascinating stranger to present itself to me.

I don't have a plan, as a rule, or specific places I need to see; I just want to take in every sight and sound, and let Beirut, La Paz, Lhasa, introduce itself to me and tell me the story of its life. After maybe two days, explanations will start to form, and then I'll see what comes to me only in the light of my ideas; but for two days I walk, just gathering as many impressions as I can without trying to force them into a pattern.

For many years, flying back to Japan from my mother's house in California, I'd stop on the way in an Asian city: Bangkok, Shanghai, Hong Kong, Saigon. Jet-lagged at home, I'd only be keeping my family up at 3 a.m., then trying to sleep while they'd be clattering around at 3 p.m. So for seven days and nights, using jet lag as a searchlight, I'd walk the streets of a metropolis all night, seeing what came out only after dark, measuring its subconscious, and, perhaps, my own.

A walk like this never grows boring: there's always an Italian restaurant open on Soi 7 in the wee hours, or some unexpected *boîte* in the Foreign Concession, serving tea and sorbets. In an upright city like Singapore, it can be illuminating to see what happens in the unofficial hours.

Here in Nara, as I make my way back through Deer's Slope, I don't need that kind of instruction, even though this place will never fully be mine. I've been here twenty-eight years, and yet I choose to live in Japan on a tourist visa, in part to remind myself that it will always be foreign, excitingly strange to me, and I can never take very much for granted.

A small dog is taking its aged owner for a walk as I approach our flat, but the dog is sporting a red coat and the owner is not. A matron is briskly heading to the local pharmacy, past the vegetable stand a local farmer has set up beside the park. We're surrounded on three sides by hills, and a wrong turn will bring me to a great bamboo forest or a line of ginkgos. By now I've come to know the community so closely that I can tell the time of day, the time of year, by the play of light and even the occa-

sional sounds (children going to school, the local bus grinding into action).

I take this walk every morning, at much the same time, and I would gladly take it every day until I expire. 'Going out, I found,' in John Muir's famous words, 'is really going in.' Even on those days when my thoughts don't go anywhere at all, there's always something fresh or surprising to see in this strikingly everyday neighbourhood, a place I could not have imagined when far away and now can't imagine living without. To learn something new – a wise friend from New York sent me his paraphrase from the American naturalist John Burroughs last year – take the same path you took yesterday.

I head up the two flights of stairs in our modest, six-flat apartment block, and go straight to my desk to take a deeper, less visible walk with my pen.

Even Greater Kailash
(and Parts of Coonoor)

Keshava Guha

India is no country for walking. In *A Passage to India*, E. M. Forster reckoned that no one knew this better than Indians themselves. He wrote of his protagonist, Dr Aziz:

> Walking fatigued him, as it fatigues everyone in India except the newcomer. There is something hostile in that soil. It either yields, and the foot sinks into a depression, or else it is unexpectedly rigid and sharp ... A series of these little surprises exhausts.

Few Indians, then or now, would disagree.

Objectively speaking, Delhi is inhospitable to walking even by Indian standards. It has the hottest summer and coldest winter of any Indian metropolis, and moves without pausing to tie its shoelaces. In theory, there are sometimes pavements, but when these aren't used as parking spaces they are frequently dug up, and resemble a surgery paused midway with the original organ and the transplant both lying on top of the body. Let's not even begin to talk about the air.

But there are really only two ways to see a city, any city: from the upper deck of a bus, and by walking. Cities aren't *meant* to be viewed from above, whether by helicopter, aeroplane or hot-air balloon; and in any case, as anyone landing in Delhi knows, for most of the year it isn't visible from above. The last double-decker Delhi buses were decommissioned decades ago.

And walking through South Delhi is a good deal less pointless than other things that some people do on its streets: such as drive Lamborghinis or keep Alaskan malamutes. Unlike those activities, walking affects no one but the walker. And as I have found over many years, while it may lack conventional charm, there are plenty of other compensations. Charm is, in any case, overrated – and uncorrelated with other virtues.

'South Delhi' refers to the planned residential neighbour-hoods south of colonial New Delhi. These were first built for refugees that arrived from West Punjab during Partition, and are still dominated by the more affluent among their descend-ants. The neighbourhoods themselves are known as 'colonies', a reminder that while South Delhi is not short of inherited resentment towards Muslims, anticolonial feelings have long passed. If Delhi is the city least loved by other Indians – only the memory of Mughal Old Delhi holding any romance – the colo-nies of South Delhi are the beating heart of everything for which Delhi is deplored.

I live in Pamposh Enclave, a colony originally developed for Kashmiri Hindus. But Pamposh is only three brief streets; no more than a phrase in a long paragraph called Greater Kailash. I live in Pamposh Enclave, but I walk in Greater Kailash. Not in the parks set aside for the purpose, but on the streets.

The name 'Greater Kailash' is a bit of a curiosity. Not the 'Kailash' (Mount Kailash, in Tibet, has been revered for millennia as the home of the god Shiva), but the 'Greater'. It's not a curiosity most people dwell on – in practice, it is always 'GK'. The part I walk in is now Great Kailash-1; but when it was first developed, in the 1960s, it was just Greater Kailash. GK-2 came next; later, GK-3 and, more obscurely, GK-4. To the north of GK-1, and within the ambit of my usual routes, is Kailash Colony; on the other side of Lala Lajpat Rai Road is the accurately named 'East of Kailash', where I was born (the area to the east of Kailash, not the eastern part of Kailash).

'Greater Kailash' ought to refer to the whole thing; and in a sense it does, standing in metonymically for all of unlovely South Delhi. In recent years, South Delhi's hipsterish minority have been hotfooting it at an alarming rate to Goa, pushed by the air pollution and ascendant heartland Hindutva, and pulled by low rents, cheap booze (now extending to craft pale ale and small-batch gin) and the languor possessed by all places where shorts can be worn year-round. A Goan friend tells me that Assagao, the village most popular among South Delhi refugees, is now called 'Even Greater Kailash'.

In the original GK, I often structure my walks around a theme. *Barsati*, for instance. The *barsati*, a one-bedroom flat on top of a house, was the product of zoning laws that limited the number of floors per building. Famously cheap, they drew young artists, designers and academics from all over India to Delhi, my parents among them. And I was conceived in one that, like most of its kind, no longer exists. The scrapping of the height restrictions instigated a construction frenzy that has yet to abate. GK is now a world of 'builders' flats'; and each time I pass a *barsati* I'm aware that it may not be there the next time.

Other walks have focused on balconies, open or closed, the latter a recent phenomenon in keeping with a time when balconies are no longer peopled. A person at leisure on a GK balcony is likely also a person whose daily exercise is a walk in the park: that is, they are over sixty. These humanly uninhabited balconies are left free for their time-honoured use, the drying of clothes; and for the emblem of India's post-1991 embrace of consumer capitalism, the air-conditioning unit.

Less often than one might like, but often enough, they are filled with potted plants. I am drawn again and again to a balcony in Kailash Colony, its plants immaculately curated and watered, which has a second row of flowerpots on a lower ledge. These pots are hung too low to be seen from inside; they are purely for the world's benefit.

Back in Delhi after six months away during the pandemic of 2020, my walks threw up the unexpected ways in which Greater Kailash was managing the new restrictions. Every evening in October 2020 I saw a wedding in preparation or in progress – in a kitted-up parking lot. New builders' flats in GK are usually four flats with 'stilt parking' taking up most of the ground floor. These turned out to be exactly the right size for a wedding with fifty guests – the most allowed during Covid.

Like other Delhi colonies, even little Pamposh, GK is laid out in 'blocks'. These begin at B, and end at W, and some letters in between are omitted for reasons that are now obscure. Running horizontally across the middle is the high street, Hansraj Gupta Marg, a pavementless medley of dermatology clinics and three-star hotels (The Grand Vikalp, Solo Victoria and my favourite, Hotel Private Affair). I have walked through each block many times, trying and usually failing to find some signs of distinct identity, some evidence that these sub-units of Greater Kailash have any meaning autonomous of the whole.

What distinctions there are occur less on the streets – *pace* the realtors who say things like 'W Block is the only exclusive address in GK' – than in the parks, which bear the mark of their Residents' Welfare Associations the way adults are branded with the quality of the parenting they received.

E Block Park, tidy but unusably drab, has been fucked up by mum and dad; R Block has been landscaped and maintained with the care and extravagance that, in India, is usually the preserve of private wealth; S Block, of any afternoon in the year, hums with warm activity: three sports in play, nonagenarians taking their constitutional, young grandmothers arguing with their wards about whether it's time to go home. I sometimes pause a walk midway to shoot jump shots while the rest of the basketball court is occupied by a game of toddlers' cricket; after a rain shower the court smells like a beach, the salty sand coating the ball with each bounce. The only perennially empty section of the park is the library, in which *Mansfield Park* sits in between Aravind Adiga's *Selection Day* and a 1998 record of Indian Supreme Court cases. Every fortnight or so I go in to confirm that none of the books have been touched.

Nowhere Is India …

When Forster wrote that India was not a country for walking, he was on to something, but later in the novel he issued an important clarification. He wrote, of Adela Quested: 'In her ignorance, she regarded [Aziz] as "India", and never surmised … that no one is India.'

A Passage to India reads almost as contemporarily in 2021 as it did in 1924, a tribute more to Forster's perceptiveness than to the country's unchangeability, and Forster never wrote a line of more enduring relevance. There is no one 'real India', and there never was.

In Coonoor ...

No one is India, and nowhere is India, too. India is Delhi, and India is also Coonoor, the tea-garden hill station in western Tamil Nadu where I spend part of each year. The population of one might be 20 million, and the other 50,000; but to say that one *is* India would be to submit to the chimera of representativeness; and to the logic of majoritarianism – the logic with which Hindi-speaking Hindu males seek to impose their ways on all other Indians.

Bertrand Richards, an Ipswich Crown Court judge of the 1970s and 1980s, once defended punishment by caning on the grounds that 'Buttocks were ordained by nature for the purpose.' I sometimes think of Judge Richards – a man notorious for the view that some rape victims ought to be blamed for their carelessness – on walks in Coonoor. Most of us have come to see that he was wrong about buttocks, and very wrong about rape, but no one would dispute that walking is a purpose Coonoor was ordained for. Every step is renewed disproof of Forster.

Coonoor is at 6,000 feet. High enough that it is rare to sweat in peak summer, and so far south that in late December the air rubs against the skin with the loving gentleness of a family Labrador. Other than the monsoon, all is gentleness; the slopes, the ground, and the drivers who – yes, these are Indian drivers

– yield to pedestrians without even contemplating the use of the horn. Coonoor is a secret that shouldn't be allowed to get out; my writing these words is criminally irresponsible.

I love walking in Coonoor; I am not perverse enough not to. But on Coonoor walks I do miss Greater Kailash and its unobvious pleasures. Walking in Coonoor is like taking a shower at precisely the right heat and density; it has a lulling effect. On Coonoor walks I find myself having ideas for novels, or mentally replaying Shane Warne leg breaks. Back walking in GK, I find myself seeing more sharply; my curiosity grows more acquisitive.

*   *   *

It may be that my inherently textual brain is drawn to street signs rather than flowers. In this regard few places can compete with Greater Kailash.

South Delhi colonies, the legend goes, were once neighbourly, with communal tandoors and friendships forged on park benches. But that neighbourliness drained away in a canal of new cars. When GK was laid out, its families were assumed to be one car (at most); by the early years of this century the average was two; now the assumed norm is three. Wars over parking offer an unheeded prelude to the wars that climate change will provoke. The one absolutely universal architectural feature in GK is a no-parking sign on the gate. Roughly half of these add: TYRES WILL BE DEFLATED.

If GK is famous for anything, it is for how very full these threats are. All South Delhi colonies have these signs; in GK they are acted upon. One corner house in S Block has six vast cars and seven tyre-deflation threats in different colours.

Close behind in abundance are the ads for internet service providers: ACT, Hathway, Spectranet, Tata Sky, Airtel, XStream, and likely seven new ones by the time you read this. For years they have adorned every tree and electricity pole. Then some ISP had the bright idea of supplying residents with no-parking signs. No ISP has had the gumption, yet, to lend its insignia to 'Tyres Will Be Deflated'; but the day is not far off.

If ISP ads are a marker of post-socialist commercial Delhi, other signs are endearing reminders that Greater Kailash is still in some sense a neighbourhood. Only someone who has walked every GK block would know that the French teacher advertising her services 'for students from Standard 6 to Standard 10' has covered every letter from B to W, and every block of Kailash Colony too, but not, for some reason, Pamposh Enclave. By contrast, the man who says 'I have some Special Techniques by which every student will be Topper in their class' has, thus far, confined his ads to S Block.

In Coonoor, houses, many of them colonial, have names that seem straight out of the *Just William* books I grew up on – 'The Laurels', 'Milford', 'Rose Cottage'. In GK they have numbers: B-39, R-211. But one in every twenty or so nameplates is more revealing. They might remind a forgetful world that the occupant was once an Additional Commissioner of Income Tax, or is still the president of a human rights foundation.

At least two Coonoor houses bear the names of long-forgotten princely states: Dhrangadhra, in Gujarat, and Lambagraon-Kangra. I have often chuckled at the tenacity with which these descendants of minor princes hold onto their claims of royal status, fifty years after India abolished titles. But right next to the GK outpost of Dhrangadhra is the home of the Honorary Consul of the Republic of Montenegro. If Dhrangadhra were a country, I realise, its population would be greater than Montenegro's – and of at least thirty other United Nations member states.

The Hug of a Husky ...

If asked why Delhi is so little loved, most Indians would go straight to the collective vices of crassness and aggression, and to patriarchy. After dark, the city is notoriously unsafe for women, but even in daytime, especially during the week, its public life is dismally male. The contrast with its rivals, Mumbai and Bangalore, is unmissable; in those cities, women are everywhere, including women working in every conceivable occupation.

It is only in Delhi, on winter walks that begin in smoke-filtered afternoon light and end in fugged dark, that I have seen women cross the street to avoid me. These are quiet GK streets, often with no one else around. They don't look back; my footsteps or my shadow or the peripheral vision evolved for a related purpose signal the approach of a man. With grim humour I think of the phrase football commentators always use when a defender heads the ball out of play for a corner: he's not taking any chances there. Neither is she.

Another contrast with Mumbai and Bangalore is less remarked upon. Of India's great cities, or perhaps one should say its enormous cities, it is only Delhi that is monolingual. When people speak of India's 'diversity', the basic unit is language. Ours is a country with no national language either by law or in practice. In Mumbai and Bangalore – as in Vienna or Prague or Brooklyn *c.*1910 – you might hear half a dozen languages spoken in a single walk. On most of my Delhi walks I only hear one. This spoken register of Hindi/Urdu used to be called Hindustani, is now just called Hindi. It takes a growing share of its nouns from English and, in Delhi, is inflected with Punjabi idiom. But it is Hindi, and it is all a Delhiwalla will ever need to know.

One evening, after eight years on and off in Pamposh Enclave, I heard two women speaking Tamil – the native tongue of every one of my known ancestors. It is another matter that, thanks to many of those ancestors working for the Raj, my own Tamil is about as good as John F. Kennedy's German. But the sound of it, on a Delhi street, was a sound for sore ears; the sound heard by all immigrants surprised by their native tongue on alien soil. I surprised myself by walking up to them and asking, in polite Tamil, 'How are you?' It is the most Tamil I have ever felt.

In Coonoor, where the lingua franca is Tamil, I feel less Tamil than anywhere, because of how poorly I speak it. But in Coonoor it is the norm on walks to greet or chat with strangers. In Greater Kailash, with that one exception, my walking encounters are generally with dogs rather than people.

Every Indian city has seen an explosion in the population of street dogs this century. One cause is the disappearance of the vultures, Delhi's traditional urban scavengers. But now – the process was imperceptible – the streets of GK are almost as dense catwise as dogwise. One cat I know is so large and his spots so jaguar-like that I have started to think of him not as a domestic cat, but as a city-shrunk big cat species – *Panthera pamposhae*. He prefers the upper reaches of an amaltas tree to the ground. Once returning home from a walk, I saw him speeding down his tree in the kind of hurry provoked by seeing one's mate in the paws of another.

I have never known how to approach a cat. But dogs are another matter. Stray dogs polarise Delhi colonies like Boca and River cleave Buenos Aires. The two tribes, cynophiles and cynophobes, regard each other with equal parts venom and mystification. As a paid-up dog lover who has also received multiple unprovoked attacks while walking by daylight in GK, I suffer from a petty but still troubling affliction – the inability to know where I stand. In practice I treat street dogs with polite wariness, and pet dogs with uninhibited friendliness.

The pet dogs of Greater Kailash (other people's) are the most sustained motif of my walks through my part of Delhi. When mentally planning a walk I – separated by 2,000 kilometres from my family dog – note with ascending pleasure which dog or dogs I'm likely to meet.

The pet dogs of GK are, as a class, mild and low-energy; it might be kinder to call them 'becalmed'. How else could they be? The vast majority are of breeds for whom exposure to the

Delhi summer is an act of pure sadism. Let's not even begin to talk about the air. Signs that threaten tyre deflation outnumber 'Beware of the Dog' by at least ten to one. In this regard, at least, the homeowners of GK are nothing but honest.

The nonpareil act of dog-lover sadism is the import into Delhi of St Bernards and Alaskan Malamutes, and their cousin the Siberian Husky. They spend the summer, if they are lucky, in air-conditioned prison. To see them out on summer walks is to truly understand the cruelty that can call itself love.

In the winter, despite the air, they revive. I am thinking in particular of one Husky, who lives with his sister in B block, home of GK's grandest houses, the kind of place where it is no surprise to find a Husky next to a Porsche. All winter they spend their days loosely tied to two trees outside their gate, accompanied by two minders. The sister ignores me; *he* always sees me coming, and by the time I reach him he is ready.

Few hugs are properly fifty–fifty. There is usually, on balance, one hugger and one hugged, and most of us gravitate to one of these roles. This Husky, whose sadistic owners I have never met and whose names I do not know, is a hugger. By the time I reach him he is up on his hind legs, and a second later two paws press tightly against my lower back. For over a year, during the pandemic of 2020, he was the only thing I hugged.

Salim Ali, the great Indian ornithologist and nature writer who did not live to see the disappearance of the vultures, called his autobiography *The Fall of a Sparrow*. Twenty-first-century Delhi, even by Indian standards, is a living – it might be more accurate to say dying – embodiment of the Anthropocene. The presence of a Siberian Husky in Greater Kailash: it is not easy to find greater proof of the absurd lengths to which we have collectively chosen to *make* rather than accept the physical world. From the fall of a sparrow to the hug of a husky; it is both tragedy and farce. But life is not lived in abstractions. And in Greater Kailash, as anywhere, to pause a walk on a winter's day and have warmth hugged into you by a long cone of fir is to feel unthinking happiness.

A Record (Rain)

Jessica J. Lee

There are days in the forest when I question my choices: my fixity, my stubbornness. Where I circle the thought that I should've gone another day, should have dressed differently, should have relented. When taking a walk is an altogether dreadful idea.

This is one of them. Rain. So much of it that I cannot see beyond the hood of my coat. It falls in sheets, vertical and sideways, on gusts of racing wind. Rain waving like laundry clipped to a line. Slick and cold and sharp. When it isn't flowing, it is pelting, stinging my eyes and slopping into my boots. Rain dribbles over my lips, and I taste salt at the edge of my mouth. Cold sweat. Behind me, as though drafting my movements, walks my dog. I hear him shake the weather off every minute, and fleetingly wish I'd left him at home in the warmth.

I've walked the Mühlenbecker Forest each season for six years, made it a record of time passing. Twenty-four seasons, the memory of each walk merging. Bright, dry, crisp. Sun, leaf, ice.

I have never known it to rain like this. The path where I have walked each summer, autumn, winter, spring, is invisible. The depression packed by walkers is ankle-deep with water. It pools where the leaves and pine needles and sand are clogged with moss. It flows in channels down the slope to meet the shore, where all the edges have overflowed.

Is their water the same, the rain and the lake melting together? Both soft and sweet, the landscape thickening with toffee-toned silt.

*   *   *

In another time, too deep to grasp at, this plateau was carved by ice, its channels thicker than those sliced by river and rain. Clay and sand record the movement of ice, such that now the Barnim Plateau, north of Berlin, stands a hundred metres higher than the sea. Unremarkable, until you see how flat the land here is. I am walking the seven kilometres from the village of Summt to Schönwalde and its single-track railway, on a trail that cuts first north through the beeches and then east through the pines. The trees change, marking the border where geology shifts: the packed dampness of clay gives way to the sponge lightness of sand.

The bus dropped me at the edge of the Mühlenbecker Forest, but no one else got off. I tried to think nothing of it, but the thought still presses on my mind: a bad day. Before I could enter the trees, I had to cross a muddy pool four metres wide. The dog had looked at me with long eyes, and I had carried him across it.

Nordic walking trails angle through the trees, signposted with little illustrated rabbits. On weekends, this place heaves with visitors, older Germans with their walking sticks and young families with their dogs. Once, I saw a Shetland pony being walked here on a lead.

But today there is no one. The tree birds have scuttled off beneath branches, and the ducks are huddled sodden by the reeds. At the mouth of the forest, I had expected it to lighten somehow, as if the canopy might make shelter from the rain. I was wrong. The leaves shake the weight of the storm erratically, tunnelling wind between the trunks.

It was not meant to rain today. By which I mean, I had not intended for it to rain. I had intended pale sun, orange light, and dry leaves. The world has other plans, I know.

But I had wanted this to be *right*. A last walk, before I leave this land for another. A moving goodbye, the closing of a cycle. Closure? A walk that was meant to look a certain way. But I ran the calendar down, and today is the only free day I have.

The first time I walked here, love had lodged deeply in my gut. It was the kind of frustrated, impossible affection that spreads itself over the places it is felt as much as it roots in the body. In all the years after, walking here, love has hung amidst beech leaves, yellow-green, and stood waiting between pines. Each time, it waned, became an ache and then an echo in the landscape. Each time, I laid newness atop it.

Summers, I walked with friends. Winters, with others, sliding along the ice-slick trail. Green unfurled in spring, and I walked alone, and then months later, other autumns came. The forest held an incalculable array of orange: oak and beech and pine together, their leaves and needles in every hue. Walking then was an auditory exercise; I came to hear the forest crackling beneath my feet. Dry and alive.

But today, I hear only wind and water. I cannot hear the land that moves beneath me.

A kilometre in, I think I have made a wrong turn. I pluck my phone from my pocket, mashing wet fingers at the screen to open the map. It shows that I've backtracked to the south of the lake, quite opposite from the northern shore I meant to follow. I'm embarrassed in front of no one, frustrated at the time wasted in the weather. I've never gotten lost here before.

My fingers twine around my phone in my pocket, poor shelter from the rain as I backtrack. I check the map every so often until the blue pulse of my body returns to the trail. There I find my footing amidst leaves afloat and squelch towards the marshland that marks the turnoff.

Draped and rusting near the tip of the lake, a fence sits detached from its posts. Here, I hang right, taking brisk little steps on my toes as the trail slides down a steep slope. The dog lurches ahead and slides to a stop in the muck of leaves. No matter; in moments the rain will wash him.

Beyond the broken fence, we balance on a board. It is rotting into the ground, but holds us atop a creek that flows heavy with the storm. I leap onto land again, the dog racing after me, and we have cleared the crossing. The ground is tacky with mud and makes small slapping sounds as I scale the opposite slope. A breath further, and we reach the heart of the forest.

*   *   *

Schloss Dammsmühle stands at the centre of the trees, a nine-teenth-century ruin atop the site of an eighteenth-century castle, built at the site of a seventeenth-century dam. The

Dam's Mill Castle. To its front sits a crooked pond, and to its back, the lake.

In 1894, the land was purchased by Adolf Wollank, who commissioned the present neo-Baroque turreted castle, plastered in pink. When he died in 1915, the property passed to his brother, Otto. In 1919, he sold it, and then it was sold again, in 1929, to Harry Goodwin Hart, the then director of Unilever. From then, the course of its history flows downward.

In 1938, Hart and his wife, who was Jewish, fled Germany. The castle and its forest stood empty. By 1940, the property had been expropriated by the Nazis, and Schloss Dammsmühle became the country retreat of Heinrich Himmler. Himmler, who led the SS. Himmler, who built the camps. In 1943, the building was expanded and renovated by prisoners from the nearby Sachsenhausen concentration camp. And then, at the end of that bitter war, Schloss Dammsmühle was occupied by the Red Army.

How much can a forest hold?

The walks I've taken here are as thick with loss as they are with newness: on the Mauerweg that ensnares the city, the death strip grows full with green, birches and trees of heaven stretching scrappy in the waste. South, near Halbe, the forest still unearths the remains of soldiers and civilians. Wartime deposits atop glacial remains: is this, too, a geologic record?

The Mühlenbecker Forest is not special in this history; the land around Berlin – once capped in ice – has long shouldered weight.

By the late 1950s, Schloss Dammsmühle came under the control of the Stasi, who used it for entertaining, for training, and as a hunting retreat. I read of parties and balls. But who could dance on such ground?

And then, as if nothing had happened in this forest at all, reunification.

Dammsmühle became a hotel, ever so briefly. And though the property was eventually restored to the heirs of Harry Goodwin Hart, it has since stood empty. Little has taken root in the decades since, as it has passed from new owner to new owner, each investor hoping to recoup its splendour but yielding at the task. The plaster peeled and the windows wasted; vines grew from the walls to the rooms, and the building began to haunt this place. Each visit, I've picked my way through its overgrown grounds, where nettles arc over the sinking pathway, where a fountain built by prisoners grows thick with algae.

Until now. As I round the trail behind the house, Dammsmühle looks altogether tidier than I could have imagined. The windows have been boarded up, and skips line the side of the castle's pavilion. A construction fence lines the perimeter. A new investor, making good on their promise. A new hotel, they say. I do not know what will stand here if I ever return.

* * *

Some things have not changed, though I know they soon will. The sign that always draws a laugh:

ANGELN VERBOTEN
Der Fischer

(FISHING FORBIDDEN
The Fisher)

Two men huddle under a camouflage tent, plying their lines in search of fish anyway. At the edge of the mill pond is an ornamental island, a ruin on its shore, all littered with the waste of some summer party. This will be tidied away, I know. And who am I to bemoan these changes? I have not been here long. Is six years enough to lay claim to a place? To lay prints in the record of the land?

The slap of pavement after all that mud. My feet hit the road beyond the castle and the shock sends my ankles zinging. No puddles here, thank God. My boots squelch out the remains of the rain. But the pavement doesn't stretch a long distance, just until the road that leads out of the forest. I am not following it. Instead, I turn back onto the trail as it curves around the mill pond, up towards the sand. Together, the dog and I track behind the fishermen and disappear into the trees.

The trees here are still green. I do not know if I am marking time correctly. Everything seeps rain, the sponge-light ground now the bottom to a temporary body of water. It flows in rivers where the trail should stand. The sand isn't doing the work of draining. The route ahead is submerged.

Another three kilometres stand between me and the station. It should not take long, but cold has crept beneath my coat. Rain dribbles from my hood to my neck, across my collarbone. I glance at the dog, who is shaking with cold. He follows me, clipping close to my ankles as I navigate the pools, all enthusiasm for our walk sapped by the water. Futilely, he shakes himself dry; his bearded face is slicked to its skinniest. He looks sad.

At the edge of the beechwood stands the foresters' pine, militarily precise, skinny and red-barked. The path stretches long and straight, into a tunnel whose end-light is dulled in the weather. As the hardwood peters out, bilberry and heather crowd the floor, their spiny branches reaching over the wet. It is these atop which we are forced to walk. I step out of the puddles and into the margin, scrambling over scrub to stay dry. And there: a crackle as I move, sticks snapping beneath my weight. It isn't dry leaves, but I had wanted a sound, at least.

*   *   *

Writing of a visit to a Finnish pine forest, the anthropologist Anna Tsing once marvelled at its tidiness. The forest was not wild, as she had imagined, but clipped clean and cold. No seedlings crowded the floor, no dead wood left standing. The forest was managed, the record removed. How else, she asked, might you stop history?

Scots pine is the most common plantation pine in Brandenburg. And nearly all the pine forests in the north of Germany are managed: clean rows of trees trimmed for timber, sprayed in neon paint to mark the edge of each stand. Once, I heard the forester Peter Wohlleben speak of a visit to the forests nearby: 'Where are they?' he asked. Around Berlin, he could only see tree farms.

These pines are derided. But they are plentiful. They stretch for miles across the sandy swathe of the plateau, across rail lines and roads, right to the edges of farm fields. Their height, dizzy, matched only by wind turbines.

I do not dislike them. If you walk a forest only for its trees, perhaps pine will be boring. But I train my gaze to the ground, in the giddy space where my feet fall. On the floor beneath these pines, I have found wonders: yellow pfifferlinge and boletes in late summer, and more species of moss than I can recount. I have spent lazy afternoons on the blanket of their floor and I will not forget them. In winters, the paths have been littered with lichen, encased in ice, and heather has grown bright despite the season.

Today is no different. I tell myself that. I hold my gaze downward as much to avoid the puddles as to distract myself from the cold. I count the sights: a record of the plants I will long for. My legs are swinging quickly now, but they generate little warmth.

We may confine these pines to plantations. But left to their own devices, they will run riot. In the poorer soils that cap this land, they thrive. To me, still, they excite.

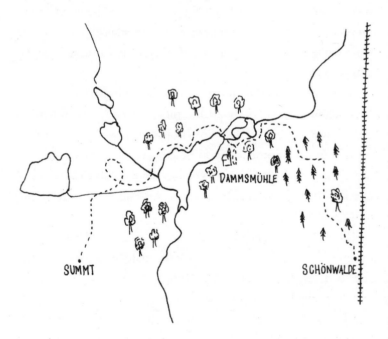

As I take the trail south, parallel to the old rail line, I pass a stand of trees left to grow ragged. The shaggy crowns hang low, untrimmed, and smaller trees – mostly seedling oaks – reach up between them. Even in the rain, through the grey mist that hangs suspended in the day, I can see green against the shadow. The ground within is made of moss more vibrant than I have ever known. Its hue is brightened by the weather. It is this, I think, that I will miss most.

I savour these glimpses, knowing the trail. I can hear traffic now and the blare of a distant train. The rain is lightening at last, but I am soaked through. I lick it from my lips and am not bothered: will I miss this storm as well?

The dog shudders and runs ahead. There, at the corner where three trails meet, stands an oak that has been left to grow long. It is an older tree than all the others, stretching broad into the canopy of pines. It is a marker I have come to know.

There, where the turnoff to the station tacks left, I go.

A Curvy Road Is Better Than a Straight One

A Child's Lunchtime Circuit

Sally Bayley

Walking takes you back in time, especially old walks, the ones you know off by heart. Walking old routes catches you out: nothing you said about it was quite true. Nothing was quite where you left it, including the child who hurries on ahead, always trying to catch up with the adult in charge, who controls the parameters of her world.

That was Mrs Braithwaite, my English teacher, who said the world is made up of words and pictures: as if we didn't know that already; as if words don't follow you around the place, trying to catch you out. Words are like stray dogs looking for a master. Use the wrong word and you sound like a fool. Call the dog by the wrong name and he will never come to you. (Any writer knows *that*.) But Mrs Braithwaite has an attitude; she thinks she's superior to the rest of us because she lives on Maltravers Drive. Maltravers Drive is *going up in the world. Very smart. Very nice. Very la-di-da.*

Mum loved the Drive for its curves. 'A curvy road,' she said, 'is better than a straight one. *Curvy roads produce a better class of people.* Maltravers Drive was one road up from ours, which was dead straight. Maltravers Drive was a *sweeping* S-shape that lay on either side of Lobbs Wood, and if you were trying to find our house (why on earth would you?), you'd walk down the Drive, nice and slowly. It's the sort of road that asks for dawdling: Dawdling: to while away the time whilst moving forward in no particular hurry. Dawdling: for Saturdays, not schooldays, for Maltravers Drive.

The Drive was on the way to school. It was as on the way to anywhere that wasn't a dump. It was like the yellow brick road in *The Wizard of Oz*, and anyone who lived on the Drive was likely to be found with a pretty wicker basket over their arm filled with lovely fresh provisions. On sunny days the people of Maltravers Drive stepped out of their houses clutching their baskets as they set off for a nice day of strolling across the Downs.

Mrs Braithwaite has one of those baskets and fills it with ART SUPPLIES. She carries her supplies around as though she's carrying around the Crown Jewels: with her nose in the air. *Art supplies* just means stubby crayons and chipped paint brushes and a few bits of sugar paper covered in a red gingham cloth. Nothing to write home about. Mrs Braithwaite is teaching us how to compose a story. Stories go around and around in circles, like a dog chasing its tail. It's half an hour before lunchtime. *Look sharp!* says Mrs Braithwaite. *Get set, children – Go –* and so we start to scribble. This is a story I remember about my walk to and from school, when lunchtime had a very short tail.

Some roads just lift you; it's a funny thing. Mum would say it's on account of her shape, because Maltravers Drive runs like a *sinuous* river through this part of town. However, if you said the Drive was a *shapely* woman lying in the middle of the road you wouldn't be wrong. You had to find a way of stepping over and around her, for the Drive ran around Lobbs Wood: a little triangle of a place, an island of green, locked inside this lovely curve. If you lived on the Drive you were going up in the world, north, not south. It was the beginning of the end of our road and I walked it four times a day, morning, afternoon, and twice at lunchtime, because Mum made us come home for lunch. We weren't allowed free school meals, because free school meals were *for the kids on the estate*, and *no child of hers will be seen dead queuing for chips and beans*. 'Chips and baked beans won't do the job, not if you want to get your times tables right. What you need is protein!' So instead of lovely cold yogurt from the fridge with curranty biscuits to dip in, I ate tinned ravioli and half-walked and half-ran with a belly full of tomato sauce sloshing around suspiciously square-shaped pasta. Try moving fast with half a tin of ravioli in your belly and wellies slipping about. Even Daley Thompson would struggle.

My Return to School Walk

Twenty-five minutes and counting $(\Downarrow)$

Walk down Granville Road to the bottom and cross over. Look left towards Irvine Road, but whatever you do, don't turn down there. *Avert your gaze*, says Mr Cooper, who runs the corner shop: from the alleyway littered with bottles; from the men weeing against the wall; from the cats tearing at eyes and tails. Irvine Road is going down in the world. *Best not look now, young lady!* Go straight ahead towards the trees and cut through Lobbs

Wood. An isosceles triangle has two sides the same length; the wood is an isosceles triangle and I cut across the bottom where the wood is shorter on one side. The dog walkers stay on the other side, where the grass is longer and the cow parsley gathers in clumps. Dog walkers are always looking for clumps. Clumps can hide a multitude of sins.

Twenty-one minutes (⇓)

At the top of the road cross the wide avenue; watch for dawdling cars: an elderly gentleman in his Ford Cortina. Off to pick up his prescription at the chemist, no doubt – he waves – why do old people wave so much when they should be driving? Turn right and you're on Maltravers Drive. The road is widening and the houses turning all leafy and ivy; red creeper around the windows and wisteria up the walls. Nothing too bare and open, nothing too much on show. Is that a woman at the window? I can't tell. Her curtains are drawn. Only the postman and gasman, or someone with a very particular reason, would dare to ring the bell.

The pavement slabs are wide here, wide enough to let dog walkers by. Dog walkers are a suspicious breed; they stand around between the trees looking shifty, making a right old mess beneath the leaves. 'Doesn't bear thinking about,' says Mrs Braithwaite to Miss Cull, the music teacher. 'The amount of dog doo-da in that little wood.' Miss Cull looks anxious – someone might overhear them – ladies don't talk about dog doo-da, especially not at lunchtime.

I spy Mrs Braithwaite on her bicycle turning down the road. She comes home at lunchtime to feed her birds – 'Budgies make an awful din, and Percy and Henry are chatty little gentlemen. Around twelve o'clock they begin to duel. If I leave them until the end of the day, they'll have pecked one another's eyes out.' Henry and Percy don't seem very polite to me, but Mrs Braithwaite is an odd sort of person; she speaks in quaint ways. She sees me and waves, in that stiff cardboardy way, like the Queen. I look busy and check my watch. I've no time for Mrs Braithwaite.

Seventeen minutes (⇓)

Giddy up! Imagine you're a Roman in your chariot whipping on your horse: Ben-Hur racing down Maltravers Drive, tutting at the bend in the road. And Roman infantry like marching down roads dead straight – bends take up valuable time – and if you're a Roman you've a got a lot of things on your To-Do List: Take Over Britain; Build Some Forts.

Now head towards the library, which you could easily mistake for a church with its tall spire; and so it was once, very prim and proper, full of ladies in hats and bonnets and men peering through their monocles. *There's a church, there's a steeple, look inside and see all the people*; but we don't have time, and a library's not a place for standing around and talking. The plaque outside says '1895': six years before Queen Victoria went underground to join her beloved Albert, her royal prince, the one she blew all her kisses to. Without Albert at her side, the Queen was all bereft. She went out riding alone, which the royal court didn't like very much. She tried walking, but her skirts were too long for the mud because the Queen was terribly short. Walking is not a good look for stout queens, so she took a walk around Windsor Castle in the morning before everyone else was up. Walking makes your bones grow, and the poor old Queen was trying to grow an inch or two; but still … thoughts of Albert were weighing her down. She looked mournfully down at the grand lake, at the leaves stuck to the royal avenue. Poor Queen: you should never look down at the ground unless you're worried about stepping in a thing or two. It's not dignified.

Twelve minutes (⇓)

I've reached Fitzalan Road, named after the Fitzalan family who came over from France and bought up everything they could see. *Greedy swines!* Arundel Castle is theirs, which you can't see from here, but it's four miles down the road: a two-hour walk if you get the map out and find your way along the river. Mr Harding, my geography teacher, would know. He's always waxing lyrical about the lovely banks of the River Arun. Old people like walking because *it's good for the joints, much better than running*, and you can go at a snail's pace while pointing at the trees and flowers like the man on the telly. Mr Harding would have us all out on a nature walk if he could, pointing and waving our arms about and frightening off all God's creatures, just like David Bellamy.

The River Arun runs from the harbour in Littlehampton to the town of Arundel, famous for its castle, which sits smugly at the top of the hill. Smugly: looking down on other people, looking very pleased with yourself. The Fitzalans were smug; they married their daughter off to the Norfolks, who were up and coming just at the right time and built their castle with a lake, where swans now sit looking very pleased with themselves. If you're a swan and you have a lake named after you – Swanbourne Lake – you'd be pleased.

Six minutes (⇓)

A walk is following a line about. You just have to decide which line to follow: the criss-cross lines of the pavement slabs, or the edge of the road where the pavement meets the gutter. Sometimes it's hard to see for leaves. The edge of the road is a sky turned sideways, the horizon lying low and flat, sometimes covered in puddles. I follow that line and start to count: the houses, the streetlamps, the grassy verge cut up into parts. Roads go more quickly when you begin to count; grey squares gone in a flash.

The Romans drew lists; they called their lists an itinerarium. Top of their To-Do List was (i) conquer Britain, then (ii) cut down trees (iii) to make straight roads through the fields and woods and hedgerows. Here's the police station, which was once on a hill – or a slope if you're being technical – and the slope is made of concrete. One summer the police decided to pour concrete over the car park to stop any roughs and toughs climbing over the fence at the back, but the concrete dried too quickly and all they caught were snails. Melissa Marshall says her dad was out all week trying to pick them off.

Melissa's dad is a detective and he's called out whenever there's trouble. Usually that means The Spotted Cow. On weekends, the Cow is filled with trouble, and everyone knows to stay away. The trouble starts in the morning, and by the afternoon they're all red and bleary and stumbling across the road to The Chocolate Box. Poor Mr Travis has to close up shop to stop them coming in and swiping at his chocolate. 'Avoid the centre of town on a Saturday,' says Melissa's dad. 'Stay away from the trouble.' It's true that if you linger too long around the police station, you start to feel like a criminal, so move on!

Three minutes (⇓)

⇒ onto the Green Lady, the lane that runs between school and town. At night, a lady in a green dress bearing a lantern runs up and down. 'Looking for late children,' says Mrs Braithwaite, 'strays and wanderers and lost souls. Now single file, please, and no argy-bargy!' There's a hole in the Green Lady, underneath the wire fence. If you're careful, you can crawl through; you might lose a bit of dignity, but you'll spare a minute or two. At the bottom of the lane is the Green Lady House. It's grand, grander than anywhere else in our town: still and white and calm. The nuns next door have their eye on it: but nuns need privacy, a high wall, and the Green Lady House has only a wooden gate that clicks open and closed when the wind blows through. I lean against the gate and wait: the front window shifts and lifts; the curtains move slightly left and right; a lady in a green dress lifts a white hankie and gently waves. Her mouth is a funny shape – it hangs loose like a saggy balloon – now it moves. 'Why don't you come in for lunch?' 'Tomorrow,' I say. 'Tomorrow I'll come for lunch.' The lady at the window has a sweet and gentle face.

One minute (⇓)

Back at school, the whistle blows, and Mrs Braithwaite starts stomping. I can see her over the fence, her whistle hanging from her mouth. She doesn't need to blow it that long, until she goes red in the face. Lunchtime is over and there'll be nothing more until dinnertime. Mrs Braithwaite looks smug and pleased, like a budgerigar pecking furiously at her seeds. Budgies are awfully greedy; they don't know when to stop and often die from over-eating. The whistle blows; Mrs Braithwaite looks as though she's about to expire; her face is so red and puffy. Did you know, 'budgerigar' means 'songbird with curvy lines' in Latin – *Melopsittacus undulatus*. Quite a mouthful. I'll practise spelling it later on my way home. Now I tread across the fields to the classroom and close my ears to the sound of the bell and Mrs Braithwaite squawking.

Walking takes you back in time: to the child who stands apart on the edge of the field, walking in circles around her peers; towards the school that is no longer there, because the Council has torn it down and left a smashed and derelict building. You walk in circles around that old route, up and down the lane, and wonder why it took you so long to get there and back; and what it was that filled your head.

Hard Shoulder

Harland Miller

I've always hated walking – though actually 'hate' is probably a bit much. An example of what my dad would call 'this lazy way you have of talking, lad', which has nothing to do with walking – being lazy, that is.

No, I think my aversion to walking has more to do with memories of getting up at 6 a.m. to deliver the *Yorkshire Post* before school.

Then again, a lot of people who had paper rounds enjoy a stroll so perhaps it's something more, or maybe *nothing* more, than one particular morning I still recall with an involuntary shudder of shame.

It was my first year at secondary school, which coincided with the 1976 Montreal Olympics. And I remember turning the telly on and banging the set to get a clearer picture of a guy – a *runner*, I thought – pulling up short with some kind of groin strain, but keeping going with a determination to finish the race by walking in a strangely exaggerated side-to-side way – which

I assumed from his strained facial expression to be the means of apportioning the pain he was in.

Clearly he was coming last and I didn't think the film crews of any other nation would be giving as much time to this single back-marker. But then it was like the British to cheer on an underdog and I began willing him on too.

As he crossed the line I imagined the rush to congratulate him was for his sheer grit. So I was amazed when it turned out that he was the *winner* and the race was not a running race, but a *walking* race; and he'd been miles out front. His name was Daniel Bautista – a Mexican.

I can only think his style of walking must have somehow impressed itself on me too, because next morning, finding myself late for school, I thought I'd give it a go. I slung my satchel round onto my back, sort of hiked myself up in my hips, and began to stride forward through the rain in that exaggerated side-to-side way, fists pummelling the air out front in a constrained slo-mo. Almost immediately I started to cover some ground – and feeling *so chuffed* I was oblivious to – well, *two things* actually. First, was that walking like this looks ridiculous, and also makes your bum waggle in a *deeply* embarrassing way – especially as my mum reckoned my trousers, which were too tight, still fitted fine. Second, was the school bus coming up behind me – and getting a load of this bum waggle of mine sent the bus into absolute paroxysms. As it splashed past, kids appeared at the windows, pointing and laughing. If one of them had been driving the bus, he'd have been honking the horn.

I never lived it down. Whenever I was spotted by anyone from the bus, I'd have to endure them muscling past me, waggling their arses. This josh went on forever and maybe that's why I began to associate walking with something sort of ...

never-*ending* … It had ended of course, and I hadn't thought about it in years. Maybe forty years. In which time I'd become an artist – a short sentence for what has been quite a slog; but anyway, there it is, and, as it was, I'd just swapped one of my prints for a Bentley.

A German plastic surgeon who collected cars and art and *my art in particular* was marrying and moving to a beach resort in Cyprus, where he intended to drive a buggy, so was selling off his cars. He offered me a straight exchange – 'a print for some plastic surgery or a car'. I thanked him, said I'd get back to him about the plastic surgery in a few years *maybe* – but for now I'd take a car.

The print the doctor wanted was titled *The Me I Never Knew*, perhaps alluding to his new life as a beach bum. But it also related to me – 'Me' – driving a Bentley. As Jimmy Cagney said in *White Heat*: 'Made it, Ma! Top of the world!' – which, on reflection, he said just before meeting an explosive end.

And come to think of it, my own euphoria after getting behind the wheel of the Bentley didn't last long either.

It was 11 March I recall, my birthday. I was fifty-two, a nothing of an age. My wife Jane was away working in Paris and it could have passed unremarkably, except I'd picked up the Bentley from the doctor's practice in Marylebone that morning and, at the invitation of friends, had set off to drive to their place in Norfolk for the weekend with my kids (I say 'kids', but my daughter Ava was seventeen at the time and my son Blake fifteen).

About eighty miles out of London I joined the M11, and unused to how smooth a drive the Bentley was, found I was quickly in the fast lane touching ninety, which felt like fifty or something. I was just about to slow down when an amber warning light appeared on the dash with a sort of downbeat 'plink' sound. And stayed on! It was the low fuel light, which looked like a person standing hand akimbo. I checked the gauge, checked it twice! Jesus, I wasn't *low* – the needle wasn't *hovering* above empty – it was lying inertly against the far left of the casing, way beyond 'E' for empty, like the broken hand of an old alarm clock. Had the doctor not filled it up? If that was correct, I didn't have a single *drop* of petrol.

The blood drained from my face down to my toes. Our *speed* – my foot feeling suddenly feeble on the pedal – *plummeted* and the car behind – now *right* behind – began flashing me. I had to get into the slow lane *fast*.

But even the slow lane seemed full of speed merchants, and after being flashed and overtaken by some fist-waving pensioners, I thought it safer to pull onto the hard shoulder and crawl along until we came to a petrol station. Or came to a stop.

'What's going on?' asked the kids, sensing this was strange, especially in this new car I'd been going on about.

'It's okay,' I called back over my shoulder – 'just … a bit low on petrol.'

Any second now, I thought, we were going to splutter to a stop. So when we came to a sign saying –

NO HARD SHOULDER FOR 160 YARDS

– that was it. I couldn't risk pulling back onto the motorway, not even for a yard.

I stopped the car, cut the engine, put on the hazard lights and fished in the glove box for a cigarette.

The first thing you notice when you stop dead on the hard shoulder is the motorway *doesn't* stop. It keeps zooming along incessantly. Zoom zoom *zooooom*. And when a juggernaut thunders past there's a kind of suction stroke sonic boom that makes the whole car rock on its suspension.

Finding a cigarette, I turned to the kids, who I realised had been asking in rising tones of concern what was going on. 'Dad? DAD? *DAAAD!!!*'

'*Sorry*,' I said, waving out the match, 'looks like we are out of petrol.'

*   *   *

As I set off walking up the hard shoulder to find a garage, I reassured myself that leaving the kids behind was the right thing to do. The Highway Code I recalled was unequivocal on this: 'no walking up the hard shoulder' – unless *absolutely* necessary. It was *way* too dangerous; and if you had to, you had to walk in the direction of the *oncoming traffic*, reason being of course cars skidding off the hard shoulder may not see you. And if you were walking with your back to them, you wouldn't see them coming up *behind* you. Ever!

No, if you broke down, you were supposed to exit the vehicle through the passenger door, and get some way away from it. In the American Highway Code I'd had to study while living there, there was even something about getting into a *ravine* if there was one. There'd been no ravine, but running alongside the shoulder was a ditch, full of rubbish, and bordering the ditch was a scrappy hedge. I led the kids down through the ditch and forcing a way through the hedge got into the field beyond, which rose up onto the side of a hill. Halfway up the hill was a tree, under which you could shelter from the rain – which had just started – *and* keep an eye on the Bentley, flashing away down there on the hard shoulder.

'Okay,' I said to the kids, 'stay here until I get back.'

'How long will you be?' they asked.

I shrugged.

I'd no idea how far back the last services were, so I'd no idea where the next ones were.

The M11 stretched away, looking as services-*less* as the North Sea. Now that I was no longer a part of it, it appeared alien and objectless, something only distance found a point to.

I felt a new panic now – the next services could be ten miles or more. I could be gone ages. But I didn't know what else to do.

As a parent I've always been fairly relaxed, which I'm not advocating is the right way to bring up children. However, it did mean that on the occasions I made a point in a very *unrelaxed* way it tended to go home, which is what I'd done before leaving them.

'Under,' I'd said, 'absolutely no fucking circumstances what-soever are you to go fucking wandering off anywhere – got it?'

They nodded.

As I retraced my steps, emerging through the hedge back onto the motorway, I was confronted by a colossal coach plung-ing towards me through the rain. *Whale*-size blowholes of water arcing up from under its wheels. As it passed, it soaked me to the skin. But I was already soaked so that didn't matter. What I was struggling with was the noise. The incessant noise!

I felt it in the vibration of the monstrous HGVs as they roared up behind me; so close I could have touched them. The rain running down my face seemed to be tainted with diesel and the taste of it had a numbing effect on my tongue as I unconsciously read the names on the backs of the containers, somehow made more mysterious in the mistiness ... ROCK PUSHER SHEETING

SYSTEMS, SOFA DREAMS and JACK ELLIS & SONS HAULAGE ... Jack Ellis! That was my uncle's name and he was always called it in full. Jack Ellis from Darlington. He'd joined the Merchant Navy and famously been torpedoed three times in the war, though he rarely spoke of it. Once, in an argument with an amateur yachtsman over some aspect of seamanship, Jack Ellis was heard to say, 'I've wrung more bloody sea water out me socks than thou's ever seen!'

In the absence of a sign for any services, I wondered if this was maybe a sign from my uncle. I pictured him having just reached dry land, pausing momentarily from wringing sea water out of his socks to fix me with a look I understood to mean 'Just get on it with it, lad'.

As the legend of Jack Ellis rumbled away, and as a nod to his fading apparition, I picked up the pace. Hunching forward, I barrelled into the headwind – walking in what was really a kind of perpetual pratfall with a permanent view of the hard ground coming up to meet me. Had the wind suddenly dropped, I'd have gone sprawling.

Every now and then I looked up for a marker – something to measure the diminishing distance by. Up ahead the motorway was down to two lanes and a sign straddling both was flashing *50–50*.

I looked down, trudged on ... *50–50* going round in my head like the sound of some perpetual uncertain outcome, and, seemingly illustrated underfoot by black tyre tracks, swerving and criss-crossing into nowhere.

The hard shoulder might sound like the endless brunt of nothingness, but actually it's full of stuff. Tyres, for sure – I was forever sidestepping blown-out tyres, old rims and inner tubes and, more disturbingly, shreds of black rubber, looking like they could never have been a part of anything fun and round, like a river swing. There were also lots of odd shoes and ladies' tights in wet piles; also a red and white soccer scarf whipped free from the window of a travelling fan's car maybe – or perhaps discarded on the way back from a heavy defeat.

At one point a lorry had shed its load of scaffolding planks across the entire width of the hard shoulder and I had no choice but to balance along one. Getting drenched as I did this made me think of … what was it pirates called *walking the plank* – 'the shortest walk'? Though thankfully my walk was longer than *that*, and when I stepped off the end, despite being splashed on cue by another HGV, I was still on dry land. Well, dryish.

When I looked up for the 50–50 sign it seemed no closer. Was it even further away? – receding as though according to some expanding relativity, the theory of which I never understood, but which made me think instead of M. R. James's disturbing tale 'Oh, Whistle, and I'll Come to You, My Lad'. A story that in fact features a man walking in rain – not down a highway but a stretch of coast, along which he is pursued by an amorphous running figure, who never seems to get any closer, but never gets any further away either …

That story – even thinking of it – reanimates an ominous sense of inertia I've long suffered from. As a kid I imagined the shadowy figure behind me to be a *part* of me – that I needed in order to move forward in life, but which I simultaneously feared. At least that was the construction I put on it when I was a teenager and, like the apparition, I've found it hard to shake off.

Walking down a highway with cars flying by created in me a new kind of *hyper*-inertia, perhaps accelerated by the possibility of being run over from behind by an eighteen-wheeler. And then all the things I wanted to do – all my plans, uppermost being to find some petrol, get back to my kids and get on our way – would be snuffed out on the hard shoulder.

To outstep this gloom, I tried lengthening my stride and immediately felt it in my groin. I don't know if this was what touched off the memory of fast walking and Daniel Bautista but, I thought, why not? The bum-waggle thing of course, *but who cares*; it was the obvious move, and though coaches were constantly coming up behind me, none of them was the school bus.

Once more, for the second time in my life, I hiked myself up in my hips and, y'know, began to fast walk. Once again, as in all those years before, I had the uplifting experience of really starting to cover some ground.

Now, every time I looked up, the 50–50 sign was getting closer.

But better than that sign was the sign – *the sign!* Ah, the beautiful coffee-brown sign, with its white border and simple white symbols: cup of tea, pine tree and picnic table, crossed knife and fork, even a bed. All one mile ahead.

* * *

One thing you don't really realise, when you turn off the motorway to the services, is how far away they still are. I think it's psychology: these days, services are conceived to take you away from the motorway, down through the gears, around a slowing series of curves and landscaped hills, into another world.

Driving, you may not even be aware of this relaxing transition, especially if you're bursting for the lav. But on foot you feel like you've entered a strange kind of manicured no-man's-land – not really intended to be walked across. In fact, as I scrambled up one of the hills, heading as the crow flies for the petrol pumps, I had the feeling that I was the first person to ever do so.

I knew, even though I could still hear the hum of the motorway in the background, that unlike a walker in the wilds, I'd never meet anyone coming the other way, as hikers do, with a nod or a 'hello'. Perhaps if the Teletubbies (which I recall my kids watching) had gone rogue and set out in the rain, I could imagine a bedraggled Tinky Winky appearing over the way – yes ... the landscape had that kind of feel about it.

From the top of the third hill, however, it was the Esso garage that came into sight. I paused to get my breath by a recently planted tree, examined my hands and knees, muddy from slipping on the wet grass. I pulled some leaves from the tree to clean my palms, and as the leaves came away all of a sudden – I slipped! Different from slipping *up* the hill, the slope was like glass and the soles of my tennis shoes worn smooth – this time I didn't just lose my footing and regain it by grabbing fistfuls of grass ... this time I went into it a freestyling medley of every type of Going for a Burton there was, from forward pitch to roly-poly. At the bottom, I got to my feet straight away, as though it hadn't happened, and found as I resumed my fast walking towards the garage that I was limping and the back of my head was throbbing unpleasantly.

I'm sure a deal of planning goes into controlling the flow of people and vehicles in service areas – people arriving tired, people leaving recharged. On the whole the system works, yet as I arrived vehicle-less, and fast limping across the forecourt, dizzy and covered in mud, I felt I was disrupting the flow somehow, coming in from a different angle.

Inside the shop, I looked around for jerrycans but couldn't find any. Joining a small queue of people waiting to pay, I was aware of darting glances and one child openly staring. But I didn't care. All I wanted was to buy a jerrycan, fill it up with fuel and get back to Ava and Blake.

Limping up to the front of the queue I was somewhat taken aback by the appearance of the girl behind the till. She was super-tall. I'm six foot one, but she was taller – six two, six three – with a mane of red hair; not flaxen, it was dyed a sort of chemical red. She looked like a cross between an Amazon of old or Batman's new enemy, taking over from Catwoman perhaps. She was certainly regarding me with curiosity.

I smiled apologetically and gesturing to my appearance tried to explain what had just happened: the car, the kids on the hillside sheltering under the tree, my wife in Paris – *my birthday* ... going on and on ... much the way I'd tumbled down the hill until I got to the bottom of it.

'... So, anyway,' I said, 'I just want to buy a couple of jerrycans, really, and I couldn't see any.'

'... Er – yeah,' she said in an even but not unkind voice. 'I don't think we've got any ... Let me see.'

She came around from her side of the counter and went to browse the same shelves I'd already checked.

'No,' she said, returning to where I was standing, by some fan belts and L-plates.

'I'll have to go ask someone.'

I nodded.

I hadn't considered what I'd do if they didn't have any. I must have looked very deflated then because she asked if I'd like to sit down while she checked out the back. I nodded again, my appearance I conceded was unexpected, but I hadn't realised it was *worrisome*. It must have been, though, because while I couldn't say she helped me to a chair, there was definitely the sense of a hand at my elbow.

While I waited, I saw behind the counter a CCTV screen flicking to different parts of the forecourt and surrounding area, including what looked like the hill I'd just fallen down. When a motorist walked diagonally across the forecourt – his head filling the screen prior to entering the shop – I realised I must have actually appeared somersaulting into the top half of that screen and fast walking towards the door.

Perhaps anyone monitoring the screen had wondered at this display, and what they might be dealing with! And there was I thinking nobody was watching. In fact it was all caught on camera, relayed in the same grainy footage as the '76 Olympics had been to my TV set in Yorkshire, but without the audience of millions, or the rush to congratulate me the way Daniel Bautista had been as he'd taken gold. When I'd entered the shop, I'd been met with furtive looks and the one child staring – at what, though? No doubt they thought they were looking at a loser. Not knowing they were looking at the current leader of the M11 hard shoulder 'somewhere to somewhere' round-walking race!

When the girl with the flaming red hair returned and *presented* me somewhat triumphantly with a jerrycan ('Last one,' she said), I thanked her profusely, and though it was green and plastic and empty, with no particular weight or heft to it – I accepted it like a golden trophy.

* * *

Postscript — or, as you might say, footnote:

It's my experience that when you don't know where you're going it takes a lot longer to get there. I don't mean that to sound like a bumper-sticker proverb — simply that I had walked about a mile or so to get petrol that day and a mile or so back; say, three miles in all. But the walk *back* went much quicker. And when the kids saw me approaching, and appeared from under the tree, actually running down the hill to meet me, I felt — as any parent whose children are growing up and scarcely running to meet them any more would feel — that the whole walk had been, well ... worthwhile.

Grain ... Again

Will Self

To my sleepless and sore mind, late at night, I apply this balm: a vision in which I am always either walking to the Isle of Grain, or am already standing on its whale-backed and scrubby immensity, staring out across the Thames Estuary. I'm poised in my mind's eye, feeling the breeze salt-smack my face and the exhaling warmth of a sun that's settling itself down definitively to the rear, to the west, and in the past ... The cats' paws scratching the glaucous waters drag my eyes across the estuary to the smudged line of Southend's mile-long pier – then beyond it, to the low smear of Foulness Island. There's no sign from this distance of the Broomway – the ancient track across the tidal flats, formed by bundles of the shrub sunk in the mud; but then it's almost impossible to see it when you're standing right on the evanescent thing, confused by this great wet-streaked plain, stretching upstream to where the chimneys of the flare-stack at the Coryton oil refinery on Canvey Island form the real eastern gateway to that city which Marlow, the protagonist of Joseph

Conrad's *Heart of Darkness*, describes as 'one of the dark places of the earth'.

I've walked the Broomway – sucking and slopping out from the shore of Foulness, ignoring the hysterical signs warning of unexploded shells, and adjuring you to not do precisely this. I've walked the Broadway and experienced its elemental conundrums – sea in sand, sand in sea, sky in both – but I'm not sure I'll ever walk it again. Foulness has been an artillery range since the First World War – a place exploded out of southern England altogether, and into some alternate universe: to visit at all you needs must call the landlord of the only pub, so he can inform the security detail at the Landwick Police Lodge, who will let you cross the bridge over the River Roach and on to the island. Either that – or you can arrive by boat, and walk its footpaths. Here, the intensification of the landed interest has reached its natural apotheosis: if you exercise some mad – and entirely notional – right to roam over the sunken wheat fields, you risk your life. *Get off of my land!* the demiurge cries, and the straying walker is blown to smithereens. Crows rise from corrugated iron bones of a derelict barn, slapping the evening air with their oily wings.

You can understand why Foulness doesn't call me back – yet Grain, its twin on the south side of the estuary does, again and again. I first visited it in the summer of 1987 – and since then have returned almost every year; around a decade ago I began to circumambulate the peninsula (the isle, strictly speaking, is only the nub end of the Hoo Peninsula, separated from the main by Yantlet Creek), starting at Gravesend. I've managed most of this – the distances aren't huge, and the going not that rough; but my discontinuous approach, going down every year or so to walk another ten miles, has resulted in the place becoming the sort of topographic equivalent of an earworm. Neuroscientific research – the Holy Writ of our resolutely materialist age – suggests that when we can't get a tune out of our head it's because we've been interrupted while listening to it, and are seeking to remedy the deficiency by incontinently repeating it in the confines of our own head.

From earworm, then, to my version of songline: the union of landforms and poetry that allowed the Australian Aboriginals to map their entire island continent, entirely on foot, before the arrival of either a single theodolite, or a single blue eye to squint through its aperture. My interrupted progress around the Hoo Peninsula has left me in this state: ever on the brink of a return I am compelled to imagine in the minutest detail. And this I connect to another insomniac writer – Charles Dickens, who, in 1856 bought Gad's Hill Place outside Rochester, which is to the south of the peninsula, on the southern bank of the Medway. He'd seen the house as a child, with his father John, whose hortatory remark that if Charles 'made good' he might end up with something similar, fuelled his ambitions. But made good or not, there was no repose for Dickens either; who often, in the years he lived at Gad's Hill, once walked overnight from his London residence, covering the thirty-odd miles in a few hours; driven on by his own relentless cerebration, as he – by his own account – composed reams of verse in his head.

England is a land softened and contoured by literary allusions. Every stream and grove swarms with fictional characters, as if they were papery naiads and dryads rustling in the wind. But the coincidence of three particular fictions that are set in this place makes the Hoo Peninsula a sort of microcosm of the country, one fashioned for me alone. The great French literary incendiary, Louis-Ferdinand Céline, spent time as a young man in Gravesend, and set a long section of his novel *Mort à crédit* ('Death on the Instalment Plan') in its environs. For Céline, the English provinces are no more or less worthy of his spleen than any other place – but he, too, was evidently taken by the Hoo Peninsula's silt-soft and eroded ambience; by its achingly void skies, beneath which villages and towns cowered. His trademark ellipsis-bedizened texts ... seem to parenthesise at once the gaps ... between estuarine things, and the closeness of their fit: as Conrad puts it – 'the sea and sky were welded together without a joint.'

Beginning before the Borough Market in Gravesend, the walker endures the salt-stung wet slap of the wind – and stares into the terracotta face of the statue of Victoria tucked beneath its wooden roof. His limbs long for the open way, hers are swagged in robes so she's both of clay and swaddled by it. Thus she is the primordial woman, born of the foreshore. Down through streets of stuccoed Victorian villas, and odd terraces set into the ground ... worn-down teeth in a cranial town – for it's empty on a weekday. Then, along the shore, through a small recreation ground, Tilbury Fort across the river hunched and lowering ... narrow corrugated iron defiles and the metallic barking of dogs as they rip at and otherwise torture the shimmery pale-blue daylight. *What're you doing here ...?* is surely the most fundamental of accusations – and it's one I've heard often during my circumambulation, from men in pickups, men behind chain-link fences, and men painting caravans up on breeze blocks.

What goes on in the windswept hinterlands of Hoo and Grain?

The very monosyllabic nature of these names hints at a certain brutality. 'Hoo!' an exclamation – 'Grain' a staple; cut and then shut together – like rusting old car bodies – they form at an odd elision: a place where the basic necessity of life is astonishment. *What're you doing here?* being the travellers' equivalent of *Get off of my land!* which is a warning in no way gentle, or measured. Warned off by the travellers camping along the ragged shoreline by Stoke Saltings, or confronted in the desert of weed-choked hard standing where the oil refinery used to be, by men I suspected of operating a clandestine methedrine lab – it was not the time to cavil. Because this region is as much about prohibitions, invisible boundaries and hidden depths – moral as well as muddy – as it is about avocets scratching across the mudflats like living quills or the principles of ethology inscribed on the vapid skies by murmurations of swifts inland, and those of dunlin along the shore. Wave upon wave of their little aerial bodies, wind combed. Coleridge coined the term 'esemplastic' to describe these, the fusing then fissioning that reminded him of thoughts coming together to induce the human mind, as much as birds flocking.

Yes: that's the way to get going, out along the shoreline path, pursued by canine barks and human bites – out alongside Eastcourt Marshes, then Shorne Marshes – past the Shornemead Fort, then on to Cliffe Fort. At each curve in the tidal river there's a pinch point – a narrower defile to be straddled by shot and shell; ordnance never fired, of course – these grassed-over batteries are the earth-girt versions of the Maunsell Forts: gaunt and now rusting gun platforms, raised up on sets of four sea-weedy legs that canter along the coast some ten miles offshore. There are small herds of these off Harwich – then all the way around the big bite of the estuary, to Margate in the south. They are the biggest waders of all upon the shifting sands of the German Ocean: bellicose phoenixes, resurrected twice daily. Beyond Cliffe Creek the river opens out still more, while marching landwards towards the solitary walker comes another tetralogy: four ranks of concrete structures, four in each – each comprising four prefabricated and pre-stressed walls and a flat roof. They, too, have the unmistakable aura of the First World War about them – that great work of technologically reproduced death-dealing. Out beyond Blythe Sands, a freighter is slipping seawards on an ebb tide, its deck piled high with white goods.

If the Maunsell Forts are zoomorphic, it's difficult not to think of England as an anthropoid figure crouching in the Atlantic – harder still, once this figuration is achieved, not to see the Thames as an alimentary tract of some sort, out of which is being evacuated the waste products of our oh-so-wasteful society. Piled up above the solitary walker is a Cubist assemblage of washing machines and dishwashers and dryers and stoves – all bound for points east, where they'll be refurbished and reabsorbed into some other body politic. Made in China … recycled in China – the only part played in this go-round by us is … entropic. And behind the freighter comes a low-riding raft of garbage containers, en route for a landfill on the Essex side. For a while the walker keeps pace with the detritus – but then it gets the better of him, and he turns inland to Cliffe, intent on an early half of gassy lager at the pub … pork scratchings and a piddle in a gents where a cistern … piddles.

On along the spine of the peninsula – from up here the landscape feels more conventional: this is what should exist in the English imaginary, not dark places, or indigestible machinery, but small fields, flinty cottages and harled houses. This is what shocked me on my first visit to Hoo and Grain: one moment I was standing in Mayfair, in central London, when I was visited by an epiphany: I realised that although I had been born in Charing Cross, right beside the Thames, and had lived my entire life in a city through which the river runs, I had never been to where that river meets the sea – and nor did I have any mental picture of this place. On that occasion I came by car, and drove in a bumbling way – no map-reading, rather feeling my way east through Erith and Dartford. The vision I had in my mind was greyly diaphanous: Conrad's welding, once again – but what I found, when I stepped out of the car, were the bulbous and castellated towers of Cooling Castle, bound by convolvulus and guarded by sentinel nettles – and what I saw then, and have seen many times since, was sunlight falling on green fields, and the Thames at high water, edged by green banks: a determinate river in a determinate landscape.

On foot, St James's Church is only a couple of minutes' walk from the overgrown fourteenth-century hulk, yet each footstep propels the walker back into that mythopoeic landscape, lit up by literary fulgurations. A contemporaneous structure, squat and flinty, St James's provided Dickens with inspiration for the first great set piece of his *Great Expectations*: Pip's encounter with Magwitch, the escaped convict. I first encountered the graveyard, with its children's tombs, unaware of its status – or of their decrease in number (there are, in fact, thirteen of them), a fictive reduction in the death rate. Pip knows them as the graves of his dead siblings, attended by his parents' headstones: 'five little stone lozenges, each about a foot and a half long, which were arranged in a neat row'. He communes with them, imagining, or rather – 'religiously entertain[ing] that they had all been born on their backs with their hands in their trousers-pockets'. So, Pip's siblings stand looking out over Grain for an eternity, perhaps – just as I am always walking there.

There's no sense of the bucolic in Pip's own view of Grain, the apron of which spreads out beyond and below the modest ridge capped by St James's. He sees: 'the dark flat wilderness beyond the churchyard, intersected with dikes and mounds and gates, with scattered cattle feeding on it'. But then Pip's childhood is effectively pre-industrial, one in which he was 'raised up by hand', while walking as a matter of course. The distant ancestors of those freighters piled high with white goods were the prison hulks – decommissioned ships, built for the wars of the eighteenth and early nineteenth centuries, which in successive decades were moored in the estuary, each with its cargo of damaged human goods. We chuck away Miele and Creda – they dumped Magwitch and Compeyson.

And on: holding the ridge for a while – mounting the giddy height (sixty-five metres above sea level) of Northward Hill, then dropping down through scrub and furze towards the shoreline once more, and along the coastal path to the living death that is Allhallows-on-Sea. Which is not to say that Hoo and Grain are so isolate they're devoid of people. But on the perpetual Tuesday afternoon I find myself, either notionally or actually, circumambulating the peninsula, there are only whitish blurs behind windscreens, the aforementioned minatory encounters – and these: off-season and immobile mobile homes in tombstone ranks, their blank windows bleared by net curtains staring sightlessly at the gunmetal waters of the estuary and the pewter skies welded to them. The first few times I walked to Allhallows I managed – God knows how – to repress its morbidity – the name itself: the night when the spirits of the dead stride forth; and the redbrick pub, the penultimate building before the short high street buries itself in the dykes and mounds and gates of the marshes, is called The British Pilot, as if to summon a very particular sort of Charon to welcome the valedictory retirees aboard, and ferry them to Southend, or Sheppey ... or Hades.

As I say: the first few of my fugitive selves die out here with the demountables – fading to grey like the after-images of walking men photographed by Eadweard Muybridge in the nineteenth century. Because it's here, a mile or so east of Allhallows, that the land itself terminates in the blunt porpoise-brow of the peninsula. (At Yantlet Creek, where mud cleaves mud while rushes and grasses shush the onshore breezes, there's a memorial marking the end of the City of London's jurisdiction over the estuary ... *for this too has been one of the dark places of the earth*. The shoreline is tendentious, leading the eye – and behind it the mind – into the immensities of sea and sky, the irrelevances of individual lives, the *sluaghs** formed by captious

* Hordes of dead souls that take the form of flocks of seafowl according to Irish and Scots mythology.

gulls. It's only two or three miles across this debatable land to
the village of Grain – but just as I can't imagine my own death
when I'm in Allhallows, so, striding along the dykes, or dropping down into the marshes, I always manage to get lost between
the two settlements – to have to double back, and meet my
fugitive self once more. I've stumbled on more than one occasion into the danger area encompassing Grain Marshes, and
wondered: what is it, this elective affinity I seem to have for
unexploded ordnance, and for the hulks of decommissioned
gun batteries?)

The Thames Estuary is – as I think I've managed to convey by
now – a passage through which much has been evacuated and
many have passed. It is also a passage of ingress to the body
economic – although no longer to the politic one: the business
people fly into London City airport, their jets describing
arabesques over Foulness and Grain, while their gazes flick back
and forth across handheld screens, but seldom – if ever – divert
through the plastic window. And striding in dream or reality
along the dyke edging Yantlet Creek, it's this, the under-im-
agined quality of the landscape that impinges on me, again and
again. The white goods are unloaded at Tilbury, ready to have
projected on to them our warped human relationships – and
then, all used up in this regard, they're reloaded and dispatched
to the East. But on Grain itself, the couch grass still grows up
between cracks in the immense and fragmented plain of
concrete left behind when the oil refinery stopped blackly …
gloopily glugging in the early 1980s.

A fragmented and overgrown plain – and one which, when I
first walked here later that same decade, remained covered with
snaking and coiling pipes, all rigid as corpses. The power station
beyond the village of Grain was built, in part, to burn the oil

refined here – but this little symbiosis, predicated on environmental destruction, came to an end in the 1990s; and in 2016 the power station's main chimney was demolished. This mighty gnomon was the still point around which all perceptions of Grain had revolved – at 244 metres high it was the tallest structure ever to've been demolished in Britain. I didn't manage to see it fall – although I'd wanted to; and now its staggered shutting-up into a cloud of dust and smoke has been incorporated into my repetitious reverie.

The giant turbine halls of the old power station have been demolished as well – while nearby, Kingsnorth – a yet more contentious site of massive GHG emissions – stopped generating forever in 2012. It was Kingsnorth that attracted the most puissant of the protesters: Greenpeace activists who scaled its giant chimney and spray-painted on to it a single name: 'Gordon ...' The intention had been to complete the phrase with '... bin it' – an injunction to the then Prime Minister to rule against any renewal of the facility. In the event, this did happen – and now, the southern fringes of Grain are bedizened with the remains of these three gargantuan enterprises: a profane trinity autocannibalising their own detritus. Across the estuary of the Medway lie Sheppey and its principal settlement, Sheerness. I once bought a concrete stegosaurus there, at one of the enormous garden centres, which, together with high-security prisons and the port, are the island's economic lifeblood.

But what of Grain itself? The eponymous hero of its own island story, the village is an unlovely thing, for the most part 1960s and 70s low-rise accommodation built for the power station and refinery workforce. But the work has, for the most part, gone – and what people one sees, walking from their fake Regency uPVC doors to their rusting cars, have the invisible shroud of poverty wrapped around their shoulders. I stumble into this settlement again and again along West Lane – and every time I do, I think: why not? Why not settle here, at this little local ultima Thule, this bitten-off nub end of England? For isn't Grain a synecdoche in a synecdoche in a synecdoche – and haven't I taken up ownership of it, by cause of walking to it again ... and again?

Down at the shoreline, feet gingerly placed on the seaweed-slippery groyne, I walk out to Grain Tower, another mid-nineteenth-century gun emplacement rendered obsolete by the time it was completed – but then receiving a new lease to carry on defending by the threat of fast torpedo boats. For the First and Second World Wars, the original Martello-tower shape of a squat and stony biscuit barrel was augmented by Brutalist concrete – and now it crouches between high and low tide, the obvious terminus.

Under its spreading concrete legs there's a way up into the incongruous brick hutments – but just as I can never leave Grain, I can never quite reach the old rope some explorer has left dangling down. If I could, I'd make the Tower my home – I'd squat here, and awaken once the tide had risen to a new life. And as for my body, left behind in central London – what would it now be, save for an empty vessel full of the city's darkness ...

Routes

Irenosen Okojie

The Conjurer's Deed

My dog Gogo and I find salvation in the clearing in the park, by the white gumtree stump lodged in the ground like a pale half-formed god fallen from the sky. The shadow of its felled branches lost between brushes on either side where broken bottles of alcohol, chocolate wrappers and abandoned items of cheap jewellery peek between the gaps as accidental decorations. Gogo, a beautiful, bright-eyed beagle brimming with joy and mischief, is keen to leave the house this morning. She circles me while I pull on my walking gear – dark tracksuit bottoms plus a baggy red Nina Simone T-shirt, a grey cardigan, a coat with a hole in the lining which stores an old Afro comb and a pair of white earphones – her tail wagging eagerly, her tongue dangling out.

At the park, we cross the orchard where the fruits of medlar, damson and mulberry are yet to bloom. Twenty minutes into our walk, Gogo escapes the lead like Houdini, slipping between the park railings onto the pavement. Running as if participating in the dog 100 metre Olympic final, bound for some hinterland Lassie would be proud of. How she manages this swift feat, this sleight of hand right under my nose baffles me. I am riddled with fear in the moment, terrified she will dart into the road. Even worse, I have no treats on me to lure her. I hop over the railing in pursuit. A blank-eyed, dank-haired woman in a baggy tiger print jumpsuit sporting a pinched expression crosses to the other side to avoid me. I am clearly distressed, mumbling unintelligible sounds aloud. A man driving a white van casts a pitying look my way before speeding by. Another man passing with his son takes one glance at my face then pulls the boy closer to him as though the stress emitting from my body is infectious. I am on my own in this.

I start running. I want to slip the white earphones into my ears to signal Jupiter. To tell whoever mans it that my dog has escaped the lead on a walk. I consider flinging this lead into the swell of traffic by the park or the exercise instruments, silent bystanders which suddenly appear corroded. My heart beating in my chest is changing shape inside me. It is mangled in a static spilling from the lining in my coat, shadowing Gogo's heels as she bounds ahead, occasionally pausing to sniff the ground or rummage with one paw tentatively bent, her damp nose gleaming, her golden-haired, wiry body wriggling in the distance, which causes my hands to sweat, the throbbing in my neck to feel frenetic.

I run till the stitch in my side becomes unbearable, until I am forced to camouflage behind lampposts in the hopes that she does not spot me as she pauses. I become increasingly panicked watching her snack on a partially eaten sausage, crisps, a scattering of chicken bones. Whatever edible bounty she encounters she gleefully consumes. I do not know how I will tell my sister I have lost our dog. That she has lived up to her name. How will I break this bad news with the ball of doom bobbing in my throat, threatening to breach into my dry mouth? I know this route. We walk it often. How could it trick me in this instance? I adjust. She will wear herself out soon enough. I have to exercise patience. I must keep walking towards the solution.

Eventually, we come full circle. Gogo is waiting for me by the white gumtree stump, where a sheaf of weathered newspaper with an item about old moon rituals done by women lies next to her on the ground. She stands on her hind legs in her familiar way of emphasising a point, as if to say, *This is what I wanted to show you.* As though she knew it would be tethered there all along – this necessary resuscitation about women who find ways to give themselves sustenance that I did not know I needed. She is oddly calm after that. We are small toys in the vast surrounding green, beckoning to the steady meanderings of the red and blue DLR trains winding their way through the back, the carriage windows stained with dried speckles of past rainfall.

Gogo does not run this time. I am relieved in the moment that she recognises me. And perhaps this is an odd thing but there is something about the panic, the chase and the adrenalin rushing through the body that makes me suspect I become an alien being to her during the chase. We make new weather running through this route with no instruments to rein our bodies in. I slip my hands into her collar steadily, tighten it, then hook the lead on, careful to keep my energy calm. She licks my face. We are so close to the stump that I spot the white swirls in it swimming in my eyeline, assembling into the shape

of a face. Beads of sweat slither into my eyes. The lines of the stump fragment, it splits momentarily. Golden sap from the face in the stump spills onto my hands. There is a quiet rumble in the sky as this baptism happens. As we lean into it, it feels like a spiritual cleansing.

And So the Multiverse Spills from a Shoe

Gogo and I could walk all the way to Kilimanjaro, or find a route to Yosemite Valley, spurred on by the slight wind on our backs, the receipts of the previous afternoon's adventures, a rupture in the galaxy that allows us to cross the multiverse. My sister is in hospital being weaned off medication which exacerbates her seizures. I am carrying her last frightened expression inside me like a map. Gogo can tell she is away. A little melancholic bubble shrouds her. On this walk, towards a spot known as 'the Alps' in our area, I am listening to the sound of nuns chanting in my earphones. I welcome nature's images as soft parachutes to embrace. It is spring. The fresh air is sharp enough on my skin, golden leaves gather, rustle, then disperse through our footsteps. Gogo and I are so aligned in the same rhythm, so intertwined, we are extensions of the pulse winding its way through every possible element, now and in the future. So much so that the nuns chanting seeps into her jaw's movements, unlocking something within. In my warped peripheral view, Gogo appears to mouth a Buddhist chant in response:

Om Mani Padme Hum
Om Mani Padme Hum
Om Mani Padme Hum

instead of barking.

It is a straight twenty-minute walk from our house. My body is opening up, the release of thoughts turned over this way and that fading. I sense things growing in the margins, punctuated by the chanting from the nuns and Gogo's slack jaw. Along the way, we pass a new old people's centre recently sprung up on one of the side roads where a derelict phone box with the receiver dangling down, the metal and glass frame a portal. Gogo tugs on the lead, the way she does when keen to explore something new, twisting her body to the right, drawing smiles from passers-by heading towards their day's adventures.

The chanting disintegrates in my veins. Its potency draws a squirrel caught in a frenetic dance with an acorn before scurrying up a scant maple tree on the left. A fox stops dead to watch us for a few seconds as though imprinting our image in its memory. I see its future flashing at me; a grizzly end under a speeding car wheel. It darts into the brushes, its orange coat bright as it moves towards its fate, hiding and unfurling when necessary. We pass the DLR station opposite the Asda store, where the sound of trolleys moving is a quiet din in the whirlwind of bodies. We are part of this urban environment with its secret green enclaves. We cross the traffic at the roundabout, I blink and there are cracked sirens behind the wheels rather than bodies, the traffic lights are missing. The roads are strewn with white plastic shopping bags doubling as landing pads skimming the grey concrete.

Gogo enjoys the climb up to 'the Alps', threading past bushes and labyrinthian nooks and crannies to get to the top, where it feels like we could touch the stars. Find ourselves speaking into the cosmos shaped like a shoe. It is daylight. We can see the whole of our neighbourhood and stretches of London from that height. I like this spot. It is rocky and cavernous. The earth shifts beneath us here as though harbouring grumbling creatures, restless to break through to feed on the light. At night, we watch planes flying past, leaving pale trails in the air and the ambulance vans streaking through the roads to maybe save a life. We are street disciples sitting on their wings. My body rises to meet an altitude here of its own making that is deceptive. I can see the faint outline of the cosmos shoe. The nuns crooning in my ears pause between their chanting. The pauses are ellipses which leave space for things to manifest.

We see a woman in the chasm of chaos below us. Perched on a rocky mound next to the remnants of a faded fire and a blue mattress with holes in it. She is an incantation. Her dreadlocks sport a green tint. Her amber eyes are iridescent, her skin is the hue of nutmeg. She casually smokes a cigarette doubling as a signal. Gogo whines. The woman looks up at us. Smiles. She is toothless. She raises her left hand towards us, offering us a palm full of teeth as if they are jewels. And it feels like breathing to walk to points of magic in the day, to be lured by a temptation in a derelict tiny paradise where the wild plants await a fall. Gogo and I may tumble down if we inch too far forward, into the woman, absorbed by the cosmos during a quiet exchange.

The Angling Community Club Offers Its Window

Our local angling club is tucked in the park along the 262 route towards Stratford. The lake is unexpected here, a fairly large body of water poised behind the clubhouse, the basketball court and playground area. Gogo and I like watching people fish in quiet contemplation, their green tents dotted behind them like refuges. Their lines bending to catch something surprising. The way the light falls on the water here from different angles is a series of watery prisms. I let Gogo off the lead for a bit, throwing sticks for her to find, then bring back to me. She is glorious in motion, bounding over tiny sunflowers sprouting from the ground, stopping to receive attention from strangers, curiously sniffing the odd spot that grabs her interest. After I put her back on the lead, geese amble away from the water onto the grass, stretching their necks, chests swelled as if enquiring about what offerings we brought to solidify the delicate contract between the observer and the observed. The painted faces of both children and adults hover between the trees and playground apparatus, looking like characters breaking out of a Salvador Dalí work. The children scurrying from one part of the green to the next. Rushing to and from various points, gathering found instruments before wielding them like weapons in mock fights.

Perhaps it is the swirl of this disparate anarchy that causes an old memory to resurface in the water. Gogo and I loiter by the edge, at the point where the sandy coloured stones crunch beneath our feet. We are looking at the reflection of me as a little girl, aged six, in a spotted white and green trimmed dress at an amusement park in Lagos where I went missing for several hours. I am holding a large stick of pink candy floss surrounded by a hive of people, but I do not look unsure or frightened. This image of me exists in Polaroid form; it wobbles in the water. Since the incident happened, I have no recollection of those missing hours; where I went to, whom I spoke to, what I did. Only that moments after the photo was taken, I wandered off, drifting further away from loved ones into the crowd, into the jaws of something masked in the day. Perhaps the restlessness in my feet began then. This urge to walk into things unforeseen, moments lying in wait that the body recognises only at the point of encountering them.

The Polaroid photograph in the water wobbles. My adult head is fixed on my little body in the picture. The image bleeds. Now the lake changes colour. It is the colour of pink waters in Senegal. The cartoon blushing the pink of the candy floss I held when I disappeared for over five hours at an amusement park on a blisteringly hot afternoon. I tug Gogo's lead, she rears back a little. We are on the move. I do not know if I will ever remember those lost hours of a day in my childhood. But Gogo and I keep walking towards unearthing parts of buried personal mysteries.

And somewhere between the pink lake, the tents in the sky, the fishing lines dangling like bolstered apparitions, we are still walking. Our bodies vanishing into a sweet mecca that orbits beyond the slippage.

Lost

Joanna Kavenna

Midway through the walk, I was lost. The sun faded and the moon rose, like a fire balloon. I was on a high, windy plateau, dark trees beneath, and then the silent ocean.

All sorts of crazy things go through your head as you walk. I was here for a break. This was quite a few years ago, and I'd been working in London as a temp. I was very bad at my job. Meanwhile there had been a spate of deaths in my family, lots of calls from pensive doctors bearing grim news. Reality felt quite unreal. People vanished, and this was clearly insane, but I was told it was sane and reasonable. I kept waking in the depths of the night, unable to breathe. I wondered if I was going mad.

Everyone told me I needed a break, and sometimes there's a good reason why everyone tells you something. I took a train to Paris and headed south. I called my boss so he could fire me, which he did. He told me I was lost. I said, 'No no, I've got a map.' He said, 'I mean it as a metaphor.' This was fair enough. But now I was actually lost. I am very bad at reading maps. Real, metaphorical. Actually all maps are metaphorical, and that's the trouble! I never quite understand how a neat, fixed representation corresponds to the variable reality around me. This plateau, for example. The glimmering stars, the vast sky. The way the shadows kept sliding along the grass. The way the grass flattened itself, as if it was afraid. There's a story by Jorge Luis Borges, 'Of Exactitude in Science', in which the cartographers of some fantastical place created ever-larger maps, because they wanted them to be entirely accurate. They hated metaphors. Finally they made a map of the Empire which was exactly the same size as the Empire and 'coincided point for point'. But the map was useless, and they had to abandon it in a desert.

But this was hardly the place for stories, fantasies. I was lost, I had to stick to the facts.

I was walking along the Grande Randonnée number 4, from Grasse to the Plateau de Valensole, incorporating the Verdon Gorge.

The *Grande Randonnée* or Grote Routepaden or *Lange-Afstand-Wandelpaden* or *Grande Rota* or *Gran Recorrido* is a network of walking routes in Europe.

The Grande Randonnée number 4 (GR4) ranges in altitude from 1 to 1,912 metres. My pack contained lots of cheese, bread and water, plus a sleeping bag. It was August; I could sleep outdoors.

The trail would take seven days, then I had to go home and get another job. I was actually (and perhaps metaphorically) lost.

I was reading the map by torchlight when a gust of wind sent it fluttering away. Sometimes it feels as if the universe is proving a point. The battery had died on my phone and I needed the map, even though I was very bad at reading it. I scampered after it, the shadows sliding along with me. I found it again, resting on a tussock. I picked it up, dropped it again, scampered off. It was a funny game to be playing, in the dark. The moon was smiling. My pack felt heavier than before. The barging wind didn't help. Come to think of it, how many hours had I been walking? Fifteen hours already? My feet were a problem. My boots were old and comfortable but they seemed to have developed a few holes. But all in all, things were fine. It was a clear, warm night. I wasn't remotely worried about where I would sleep. I was always happy in nature.

I'd begun at Grasse a few days earlier. Many paths lead out of Grasse. I went backwards and forwards for a while and then I marched uphill as fast as I could. There was a long view of the glittering ocean, then the path ducked into a shady forest, birds singing among the gnarled oaks. I thought I heard a lark. As night fell, I crawled into my sleeping bag, not even bothering to move it off the path. I woke again in blazing sunshine, with a family of hikers stepping carefully over my head.

The landscape was dreamlike. Cicadas chirped wildly, everywhere. The loudest insects in the world. My compass kept freaking out. The map – well, I've said enough about the map. But it was trouble, always. Day 2 was mostly about tiny flowers and magic. It was very hot, and I had to ration my supplies of water. The flowers were lovely and minuscule. So many variegated colours! I spent the whole day thinking about water. That night I slept at the base of a limestone cliff, in the middle of a circle of boulders. I felt happier being inside the circle; it gave me a feeling of security. Before I went to sleep I tried to count the boulders – seventeen, or eighteen? Or sixteen? No, definitely seventeen. There was a gap in the circle, like a doorway. I slept deeply, woke at dawn, the last stars fading in the grey sky.

Everything was cold and eerie, the gap had disappeared. Now there was no doorway, just a neat circle of boulders. It made no sense. I wondered if a boulder had rolled down the mountain in the night, and careered into the gap. Or, if the circle was magical. The doorway ensnared foolish travellers. Stone giants ate them. This was impossible, but so many impossible things had happened recently, you couldn't be too careful. I gathered my things and tiptoed out of the circle. The mountains had craggy, ancient faces. I was certain there had been a gap.

On Day 3 I slept in a forest. My bed that night was very comfortable. I found a pile of moss, and lay down. I was so pleased about that bed. It cost nothing, and the smell of the moss was rich and delicious. No boulders, no gaps. Just the orotund cries of finches. In the morning I saw a heron in a lake, so still I thought it was a figment – then it made a gliding magisterial ascent. I splashed into the lake, gulped down water. Then I filled my bottles again and set off with the heartening sound of my pack sloshing behind me.

Now it was Day 4, and I had been walking for hours, on the path, off the path, back to the path again. I saw a black shadow ahead of me, its shape indeterminate. I thought it might be a refuge, somewhere warm and comfortable. A fire, a bed. I started hurrying forwards, but it became swiftly apparent it was just a ruin. The crumbling walls provided some shelter, so I lay down on the lee side. I was glad to be out of the wind. The sky was full of famous stars and layers of iridescent dust. I was reading a book by Hubert Reeves, *Pourquoi la nuit est-elle noire?* The dark night sky proves that the universe is finite. Also, we are made of stardust. When we die, this energy is dispersed into something else. Nothing that has existed can ever truly vanish. It made no sense. I was tired, my French wasn't good enough.

The wind howled. I was asleep when someone tugged at my foot. I half-woke, assumed it was a dream. Black sky, celestial dust. I couldn't actually be sleeping in the depths of nowhere, alone. Then I heard a loud, definite rustling and then – worse – the sound of footsteps. Suddenly I was awake and very frightened. 'Who's there?' I said, stupidly. 'What do you want?' I said all sorts of stupid things and then with a desperate, trembling movement, I switched on the torch.

I expected – a murderer, a pale lunatic, a moon spirit, the ghost of my father. Instead – sheep! I was so angry with them, for scaring the hell out of me. But they looked miserable, with their little white faces. Like a Greek chorus, masked and anxious. I had stolen their bed. It was the only sheltered place for miles around. 'I'm sorry,' I said, still trembling from the shock. 'I'm only here for a night.' They stared at me, balefully. 'Why not settle down over there?' I said – gesturing towards the opposite wall. It wasn't as sheltered but it was better than

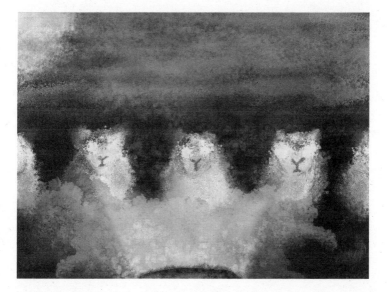

nothing. For a while the sheep stood around, then by some mysterious consensus they gave up and wandered off. I switched off the torch, my heart still pounding. What a ridiculous scene! It took a while before I slept, if timorously, and when I woke again at dawn the sheep had vanished. I hoped they'd had a decent night.

The GR4 has a system of signs, which are very helpful if you read them correctly. A white line over a red line means *Follow the Track*. The same two lines with a white arrow beneath, pointing left or right, means *Change Direction*. A red line and a white cross means *Wrong Direction*. I admired the clarity and simplicity of these signs, even though I often misread them. They referred to tangible objects in space. A landmark. The next village. The right or wrong track. Yet my thoughts were garbled at the time and I often wondered if the signs meant something else. Why did I keep finding myself on the Wrong Track, for example? When the signs said *Change Direction* did that just mean *on the GR4* or *in life in general*? The path forks constantly, and there are no signs. In life, not on the GR4, where there are always signs. Like anyone, I missed the dead. I couldn't summon them, except in chaotic memories and dreams.

A brief rest, to stop my thoughts. Misty crags in the distance. Shepherds on the path, dogs barking. The smell of lavender. More finches, bouncing on the air. I filled my bottles in a syrupy stream. A tree had been struck by lightning, its smooth trunk white as bone. There was the sign again, *Follow the Track*. It was a good path, firm and definite, and it led all the way to the Sublime Point and the Verdon Gorge. Lustrous banks of trees, shimmering sapphire waters. I dined on fish and potatoes, drank Bordeaux, slept in a campsite. Pure bliss. No giants, no ghosts.

The next day I was on the right track and so was everyone else. The path through the Gorge is named after Édouard-Alfred Martel, who carried out geological surveys in the first decade of the twentieth century. When Martel arrived, there were no paths at all. He made his own track, which was now the only track. It was hard to imagine this place completely deserted and with no trails or signs. The Gorge was stunning, but it was August and it was full of people. We moved in a sluggish queue, which stalled entirely at the ladders. The rocks were intricately shaped, like Gothic cathedrals. The only exit was far above us.

It was hot and claustrophobic. The queue paused at another ladder. I was thinking about water as usual, when I saw a man sitting on a rock. He was wearing a thick brown suit – an odd choice. He was red in the face, leaning forwards, breathing heavily. He looked depressed. When the queue finally moved, I fell in behind him. He walked with his head bowed, he never even glanced at the scenery. Occasionally he mopped his face with a white handkerchief. He took off his suit jacket, slung it over his shoulder. His shirt was soaked with sweat. He had a slender, handsome face, and grey-black hair. Above us – great walls of sculptured rock, people dotted all over them, moving uphill to the exit. I envied these tiny people far above, because they were almost out of the Gorge.

What a strange idea, I thought. Queuing in a kiln, getting boiled alive. For fun. What an experience! Nature worship. I thought of W. H. Auden, hating mountains. Well, I liked mountains, and windy plateaus, but I hated this boiling gorge. Brown Suit wasn't carrying a bag; he didn't even have a bottle of water. I couldn't bear it any longer. I went up to him, holding out a bottle. Everyone had water apart from him. I said, 'Would you like this?' He looked at me, startled, waved his hand, no no, he was fine. Thank you! We carried on in silence, I lost track of time, wondered about Auden and about this man as well. Eventually I tapped him on the shoulder again and said, in my poor French, 'Please take it, I have a lot.' This time he thanked me and seized the bottle, drank almost all of it. He looked dazed. Then a man behind me, a total hiker with all the right gear, offered me a replacement bottle of water. I was really moved by this gesture. I wanted to tell him about the signs, and the heron and the giants and how I'd upset the sheep, but I just thanked him again. Total Hiker said, 'I'll keep an eye on you!' Then he gave his water to the Brown Suit, who accepted it gladly. I thought it was funny, this gorge was hell – much too hot, rammed with people. But the people were kind in hell even if the place was brutal. Perhaps I had heatstroke. Now, thank Christ, the path was climbing upwards, to the exit. The Total Hiker had vanished.

At the top of the Gorge there was the most amazing thing: a little café selling ice creams and drinks. It wasn't even a mirage. Brown Suit spoke, and asked if I would like a beer. He was called Gabriel. We sat on a bench, drinking our beers and feeling very happy – at least, I was overjoyed. 'I'm sorry, I couldn't speak down there,' said Gabriel. He was a musician from La Rochelle. He was here because his brother often hiked in the Gorge. He died a few days ago, of a heart attack. He was only forty. The shock of his death was so incredible, said Gabriel, that he hadn't known what to do. So he came here, to be with his brother. I said I was really sorry. 'Has it helped?' I asked. Gabriel was confused – my French was not remotely sufficient for this sort of conversation. 'I mean,' I said. 'I came here, also, because I thought it might help. With my own sense of loss.' That's what I was trying to say, at least. 'Nothing helps,' said Gabriel. 'Except time. Time numbs the pain.' But he said this in a much more elegant way. 'Le temps,' he said, 'c'est une musique sensible qui engourdit la douleur.' I think this is what he said. We finished our beers and stood. Clumsily, I said that if we met again I would buy him a beer, and he laughed. We both knew that wasn't very likely. We shook hands and then, unexpectedly, we hugged. His shirt was still soaked. When we parted, Gabriel said, 'You go first, you're faster,' so I thanked him again. Then I went off as quickly as I could, trying to prove him right.

I never saw Gabriel again, not on any of the further paths. I walked along the GR4 for another day or two. Then I took the train all the way back to Grasse, went home, got another job. In a sense, that walk changed my life. But it's impossible to know for certain. It was just a few days on the GR4, a massive tourist trail. It wasn't a difficult or remote hike, except I was in such a feverish state. When I try to write 'Grande Randonnée', my computer types 'Grand Randomness' instead. My walk along the GR4 was characterised by great randomness. The path forked, over and over again, and often I took the wrong path. But so many interesting things happened on the wrong paths that I was never sorry I had taken them. My ex-boss and Borges were right. The maps are inadequate. The real journey is imaginary. Gabriel and I were both mired in grief, and yet it was a total coincidence that we ended up in the same part of the queue. Then again, perhaps everyone in the queue was mired in grief, the agony we all carry around with us. Perhaps this is part of the great randomness. Time is a music that numbs the pain, as Gabriel may or may not have said.

And walking is a strange discipline. Your mind charges all over the place. The dead, the living, the stars, the real and the unreal – everything merges and still your body commits to this rhythmic movement. Beating time, onwards. I'm older now and the path still forks. I keep walking, as always.

Portals

Agnès Poirier

I had passed those grey walls twice, sometimes four times a day, between the ages of ten and fourteen. But it was only much later, as a history student at the Sorbonne, that I realised how vertiginous my daily walking routine had truly been.

I had been told a few times as a child that the grave of a famous Frenchman, whose name adorned many streets and avenues in America, lay behind those old walls at 35 rue de Picpus, in the twelfth arrondissement of Paris. A great Frenchman and, I eventually found out, another thousand or so of our compatriots. Was it the nondescript building with its religious association, or the incongruity of what stood right opposite, an ugly-looking Renault garage built in the 1970s, that failed to arouse my teenager's curiosity? I waited until my early thirties to walk through that door. Or was it a portal? With one step, I left the twenty-first century and entered the seventeenth century, and with another, I stared at the year 1794 and its tumbrils full of headless corpses.

To walk in Paris is to constantly time travel. And to dive headfirst into a history full of dark corners and luminous boulevards, of street protests and amorous bowers, *quartiers* of abject poverty and luxurious *impasses*. In the courtyard of what is now the home of the Sisters of the Sacred Heart, visitors' feet easily trip against the uneven seventeenth-century cobblestones, and this alone, just as in Marcel Proust's *Remembrance of Things Past*, reminds one of the temporal voyages they have just embarked on. As with odours, flavours and sounds, the touch of *feet* on a particular surface or terrain leaves an ingrained neuronal trace in the brain, which is activated each time the sensory signal repeats itself. In other words, walking triggers its own chain of memories, with feet acting as transmitters to the brain.

Passing the gate of 35 rue de Picpus, visitors' feet quickly register the change of *décor* and epoch. Welcome to Picpus Cemetery, one of only two private cemeteries in the French capital – the other being the Portuguese Jewish cemetery in the nineteenth arrondissement.

Between 14 June and 27 July 1794, the guillotine was erected nearby at the Place of the Overturned Throne, today known as Place de la Nation, where I lived for the first twenty years of my life. During those five weeks of the summer of 1794, 1,306 people were guillotined; their bodies thrown into common pits hastily dug at the bottom of the Sisters' garden on rue de Picpus. Two marble plaques inside their chapel give the names of those unfortunate people who lost their heads so that the Revolution could live on and run its course. Among them many aristocrats, but also nuns and ordinary folk. Alongside the famous Noailles, Montmorency, Rochefoucauld, Polignac and Rohan families lie citizens of all ages and occupations. The long list of victims makes for moving reading: they were farmers, wigmakers, gardeners, musicians, teachers, cooks, actors, grocers, bailiffs, poets, weavers, seamstresses, even a muslin and chiffon maker. The *Terreur* did not discriminate, and the Revolution ended up devouring its children with the same rage it had the country's tyrants. So, on that snowy day of January 2008, I had come to pay my respects to a great Frenchman, and ended up saluting a thousand of my compatriots, buried under my feet.

After the Revolution, a group of aristocrats discreetly bought the plot of land where their relatives' bodies had been cruelly discarded; and, to this day, relatives of the guillotined can be buried alongside their ancestors. This is how the Marquise Adrienne de Noailles came to be buried at Picpus Cemetery in 1807. She had wished to be reunited in death with her beloved sister, mother and grandmother, all three guillotined thirteen years earlier. In 1834, her husband joined her in this last resting place. His name: Lafayette. The Marquis de Lafayette. Through him, two glorious events joined up in memory and in place – the soil that covered his grave was the earth he had brought back for that purpose from Charlestown in Boston, site of the Battle of Bunker Hill, one of the key battles of the American Revolutionary War.

As I stood silently in front of his grave, looking at the American flag flying above in the cold winter wind, I tried to superimpose in my head the black and white images I had seen of US Army General John J. Pershing and Colonel Charles E. Stanton standing at exactly the same spot on 4 July 1917, three months after the United States had entered the First World War on the side of France and her allies. And I remembered the words uttered by Colonel Stanton who, just like me, was look-ing at Lafayette's grave:

America has joined forces with the Allied Powers, and what we have of blood and treasure are yours. Therefore it is that with loving pride we drape the colors in tribute of respect to this citizen of your great republic. And here and now, in the presence of the illustrious dead, we pledge our hearts and our honor in carrying this war to a successful issue. Lafayette, we are here! Lafayette, nous voilà!

There seldom was a cry that so warmed French hearts. And with the memory of that moment, I retreated from Picpus Cemetery and emerged back into twenty-first-century Paris.

To be born a Parisian is to be born a compulsive walker. The specific geography and demographics of Paris – one of the most densely populated cities in the world, with around 53,000 inhabitants per square mile – make the city a permanent beehive where one is never alone. Every street has its artisan bakery, butcher, greengrocer, bank, independent bookshop, café, wine bar, bistro and patisserie. For any budding or young walker, this is a reassuring feeling. Later in life, Parisians may aspire to more calm and less promiscuity. However, their world views will have been shaped by this togetherness, and more often than not by this communion of spirit.

If the constant proximity feels claustrophobic, there are always Parisian cemeteries, havens of perfect balance between solitude and intimacy – only with ghosts. All in all, an attractive proposition for curious teenagers. Aged fifteen, I had a routine with my friend Laure. Once a week, during an unusually long lunch break at school, we would take a sandwich with us and roam Paris looking for mysterious places. I was the chubby blonde, she the lean brunette, and we were both strong on research. We were on a quest for singular and romantic places and the choice of our weekly excursion was based on thorough preparation.

On another very cold and snowy December day, we headed excitedly towards Passage d'Enfer ('Hell's Passage') in the four-teenth arrondissement. And from there we made our way to Montparnasse Cemetery and its main gates on Boulevard Edgar Quinet. The place was almost deserted, and with the fresh and unusually thick snow under our feet, we felt we were walking

on cotton wool. The strange lack of footsteps, the striking black and white contrast between the blinding white of the snow-covered graves and their dark grey edges, not to mention the freezing air, impressed our young minds. We had drawn up a list of the souls we wanted to pay a visit to. Laure did not want to miss the tombs of Jean Seberg, Guy de Maupassant and Man Ray. And I, Simone de Beauvoir, Jean-Paul Sartre and Baudelaire. A carved oval headstone on Man Ray's grave read 'unconcerned but not indifferent' in English. My friend and I, intrigued, tried to pierce the subtext of those four words and we soon forgot about everything else. The expression remained a private joke between us for years. And to this day, I don't quite know what we really meant when we knowingly uttered the phrase, other than a sign of solidarity.

Paris is tailor-made for both digression and forthrightness, for poets and generals. It's as if the narrow winding streets and large straight boulevards were always built for that purpose: poetry and politics. In Paris, to walk is to observe and escape, to stare and pass, and to form an opinion. After all, what is a Paris protest other than a walk in prose? A long, healthy and combative promenade, and a chance to find a way out of a dilemma. It is a process, from A to B, spatially, physically, mentally. And politically.

On yet another December afternoon, this time in 1986, I lied to my parents and went on my first demonstration with my school friends – a French rite of passage. We had no idea what was really at stake. We were, in truth, unconcerned, but I guess not indifferent. French students were protesting against the latest university reforms by the Chirac government and his education minister Alain Devaquet, and we young teenagers just joined the party. The appeal was to march – in other words, to walk – right in the middle of the street, from Bastille to Les Invalides, a glorious *parcours*, almost a scenic route. Two popular singers were supposed to be singing at the end of the demo. We began our march with the passion of the newly converted. We looked around us: the banners showed the creativity of protest – the puns were hilarious. This was a new world, and a very enticing one. The atmosphere was joyful and playful; this was what we had been born for. We repeated the slogans, there was a rhythm to them, they even rhymed. And we kept chanting: 'Devaquet, si tu savais, ta réforme, où on s'la met. Au-cu! Aucu! Au-cu-ne-hésitation!'*

Night had fallen and we were approaching the large lawns in front of Les Invalides, where Napoleon's tomb stands in majesty. Suddenly we smelled tear gas. What was happening? We could feel the tension in the air and we knew it was now a time for adults, not kids like us. We rushed to the nearest *métro* with a mixed feeling of dread and elation; we did not tell our parents where we had spent the afternoon. The morning after, we heard them talk of a student, Malik Oussekine, who had lost his life when the demonstration turned ugly, and we realised the meaning and importance of politics. Three days later, the government accepted the students' demands and withdrew the reform. This was the first of many Parisian demonstrations I took part in over the years and decades – how to resist the temptation not only to express one's opinion but also, just as importantly, to walk in the middle of the street with the heady feeling that you own and rule the country with your feet? This very Gallic pastime has since conquered far-flung places. Half the world now seems on

* This loosely translates as: 'Devaquet, if only you knew what we do with your reform. We use it to wipe, to wipe, to wipe our ass.'

the streets: from Hong Kong, Ukraine and Belarus, to Chicago, Buenos Aires, Moscow and Amsterdam.

Walking, of course, is a profoundly European experience. And it would not be a quintessentially Parisian trait if it was not primarily ingrained in Europe's DNA. Long before the train and the automobile, Europe was trodden by and large by foot. If custom duties might have limited trade between European countries, and wars hindered free movement at certain periods, the European landscape lends itself perfectly to walking. Even across the Alps, Europeans have been able to intermingle freely. From Roman roads to hiking trails, from pilgrimages to invasions, the idea of Europe rests on walkable horizons.

If you can take Parisians out of Paris, and Europeans out of Europe, you cannot take Paris out of Parisians nor Europe out of Europeans. Some habits die hard. A born-and-bred Parisian and European walker will never baulk at discovering other cities by foot, even monstrously large ones such as Tokyo, or walker-unfriendly ones in the United States. They insist on keeping their habit of walking everywhere, wherever they find themselves. For them, it is one of the best keys to understanding other people and other cultures. In an unknown and new environment, it is also a profoundly empowering experience.

As a young Parisian woman wandering Paris, a *flâneuse* by choice and by passion, I found a way to tame the city and its streets. Learned how to avoid their many dangers, and deal with fear. It was a school of life.

'Faraway Places Near Here'

In Search of Maeve Brennan

Sinéad Gleeson

1

In the past, I have written about spectral encounters but have never actively gone ghost-hunting. Chasing the dead might verge on too melancholic for some, or – in the whirling dervish world we occupy – amount to a waste of time. In 2013, I set out to retrace the steps of Irish writer Maeve Brennan in New York, a city with ghosts on every street corner. Just as Emily Dickinson readers flock to Amherst, or the Brontë faithful make for the moors of Haworth, my pilgrimage was to Manhattan. Not in search of blessings or basilicas; but to move a little in one writer's orbit and explore the streets of her past. Brennan had a way of gauging the metric of loneliness in a city, and capturing what it is to be a woman moving around a metropolis. My walk was more an act of veneration than resurrection, to see if I could find her across the decades, lurking in the circuitry of New York's blocks.

2

Maeve Brennan was born in Dublin in 1917, on 6 January, a date that has literary associations with a more high-profile Irish writer, James Joyce. The date is the setting of 'The Dead', the staggering crescendo to *Dubliners*, a short story collection that never stands still. Joyce was a kinetic writer; his work meanders all over his home city, most evident in *Ulysses*, the ultimate perambulatory novel. On the other side of the Atlantic, Brennan moved around New York, writing about the sidewalks and restaurants, the people and their glorious, odd lives. Walking – *flâneuring* – was central to both, and unlike many Irish writers of the past, Brennan and Joyce were savants of cities and streets, not fields and farms.

3

New York is pure possibility. A beacon for immigrants and travellers, a place where you create your own narrative. Whenever I've been here in the past decade, it's been for work and my schedule mimicked the pace of the city: twelve-hour days, no galleries or tourist spots; but on this trip, I carved out a day to go in search of Brennan. I compiled a list of places she lived and worked: the bars and restaurants she frequented, the many neighbourhoods she orbited (Angela Bourke's excellent biography *Maeve Brennan: Homesick at the New Yorker* is a trove for this). Brennan's own writing is full of maps and dropped pins: the exact address of her Dublin childhood home features in several short stories, and many Manhattan addresses appear in her columns for the *New Yorker*. Greenwich Village and Midtown form two distinct clusters, so I start in the former, resolving to move up the spine of this crammed island.

4

In 1954, the first of Brennan's 'Talk of the Town' columns appeared in the *New Yorker*. She was the first woman to write for the coveted slot, and wrote as 'The Long-Winded Lady'. While her fiction is minutely interior, these pieces were narratives of the outside; of the urban, unknowable place that is the city. As one of millions of New Yorkers, she moved unseen among her subjects. On the street, no one knows that you're not from that place.

5

Walking is the body in action on the street. *Left, right, left, right,* lungfuls of air, arms swinging, the heart's stopwatch tap, tapping away. I move along the sidewalk stepping in and out of shanks of light, attuned to its rhythm.

6

My hotel is in the heart of Maeve's beloved Greenwich Village. It's small, with dark rooms, and an ancient elevator that feels like it will stall every time I set foot in it. Of all her addresses, the one I most want to see is minutes from here, but I hold off, allowing the possibility of it to hang over the day. The walk to Washington Square Park is soundtracked by the busyness of the city. The chaos and traffic and overheard phone calls clashing and harmonising, pleasantly discordant. No other city sounds like it. The park is announced by its famous arch, built to commemorate the inauguration of George Washington. New York is fond of its tall landmarks but this one is more subtle.

Made of white Tuckahoe marble, it apes European victory arches. Maeve Brennan must have passed under it hundreds of times, as she walked her dogs here. Inside, rows of cherry blossom clutch pregnant, pink buds. Brazen squirrels skitter on the paths, undaunted by the volume of people. A group of chess hustlers have games lined up on tables and the public can pay to play. Behind them is Hayden Hall (now an NYU dorm), formerly the Holley Hotel where Maeve had a room. Brennan lived in countless hotels and apartments, never staying long in one place. In a 1962 piece, 'Faraway Places Near Here', she outlines multiple addresses: Sullivan Street, 22nd Street near Ninth Avenue, Tenth Street, Ninth Street near Fifth, Hudson Street – all on my map. Tiny rooms dominated by huge fireplaces, where the nomadic Brennan stayed short-term. She called herself a 'traveler in residence', and it was said she could fit all her possessions in one taxi. Looking up at Hayden Hall, I wonder if, back then, she had a park view? Or (like my hotel) a room that looks onto a yard or the bland windows of other guests.

7

Back under the arch, leaning into the March wind I walk up Fifth Avenue, veering left onto West 10th street. Maeve lived in at least two apartments on this street, and such was her love of specificity and setting it became the title of a story, 'The Door on West Tenth Street'. It's quiet, dotted with trees, and No. 27 has an impressive front: a red wooden door framed by a black pediment and two ionic columns. It's suggestive and mysterious in the way Brennan often gave places a sense of personhood. Streets took on traits of their own: Park Avenue, she wrote, wore 'such an air of vast indifference to humanity'. In one piece, Broadway is 'selfish', and in 'I Wish for a Little Street Music' (from 1968), she describes it as 'dying'.

8

I once found myself here to make a radio programme and took a walk around Manhattan with the writer Teju Cole. In his novel, *Open City*, a character moves around New York on foot, and Cole says it was massively influenced by *Ulysses*. We wandered Nolita and talked about the importance of looking upwards in the city; not to the glassy condos or corporate skyscrapers, but to each shopfront or café, as a window into the past. Cole believes that places carry traces of what happened within and that we – as viewers and walkers – should attune ourselves to that vanished history; to things no longer visible, but 'still part of the spiritual atmosphere'.

9

Cities *need* to be walked: you lose too much of the experience on the bus or subway. I learned this lesson one sticky summer in London, taking the Underground around the vast network of tunnels. IRA bomb scares were still a regular occurrence and one afternoon the Tube was evacuated when I was two stops from home. Emerging from King's Cross Station into the hot sun, disorientated, I discovered that I didn't know how to actually get around the city on foot. In New York, there is too much to miss out on if you're coiled up in an airless 4, or 5, or J carriage. Even if you avoid them, the trains are a constant presence, growling under the city with a steady, subterranean beat.

Above ground, New York is torrential – pedestrians, traffic, hurtling in all directions, hard as rain.

The New York street grid dates from 1811 and locating oneself is a matter of following its linear mathematics. Above 14th, the streets are aligned with the run of the Hudson River, rather than cardinal north to south, or east to west. It's an instant map for any walker, but easy to miscalculate distance when buildings take up an entire block. Once, after a sleepless overnight flight, I stepped out of the stewed air to walk the rest of the way and get my bearings. I underestimated the length of the blocks and ended up dragging a suitcase with a misbehaving wheel forty minutes in sweltering heat. Another night, on a twenty-block walk to the home of two writers, Manhattan was heady, almost cinematic. A man appeared, trundling a rail of clothing to some unknown location, a driver and female pedestrian engaged in a screaming match, and two men on a corner – lovers – leaned into each other, whispering, urgent.

10

These journeys had a reason, but a walk does not require a purpose. In 'Street Haunting: A London Adventure', Virginia Woolf uses the procurement of a pencil as a means to get out into 'the champagne brightness of the air and the sociability of the streets'. She argues that this urban immersion is a means of losing oneself in the lives of others, something also evident in Brennan's non-fiction. Her walking was unmapped, usually for the hell of it, but it provided the material that, to me, is her best work. Given the peripatetic nature of her life, Brennan did not have a familiar door to return home to, as Woolf did. 'Street haunting' has a duality too; the individual haunting the streets, and the city itself haunting the individual.

11

The route to the second group of Maeve's haunts is punctuated by two of Manhattan's most famous structures: the lean wedge of the Flatiron Building and the shimmering exclamation mark that is the Empire State. A few blocks up, the New York Public Library looms, where Maeve had her first job. I picture her among the spines and reading lamps, biding her time, waiting to write about her adopted city and all she encountered within it. I move from the NYPL across to Bryant Park – another of her favourite spots – and its vast carpet of spring tulips. Outside the gates, Brennan once spotted a three-cornered shadow on the ground which jolted something in her: 'I recognized it at once. It was exactly the same shadow that used to fall on the cement part of our garden in Dublin, more than fifty-five years ago.'

Overhead today, the sky was a bank of pewter cloud, with no strip of sunlight to replicate the corner of a Ranelagh garden. Instead, I turn in the direction of The Algonquin, two blocks away on West 44th Street. After she joined the *New Yorker*, Brennan frequently held court there. In one 'Long-Winded Lady' column, she writes of seeing Julie Andrews shooting a film in the hotel. Brennan watches the actress eating a sandwich, 'her hungry face glazed with anger'. This was her gift: noticing someone in an open, vulnerable moment, and transferring that act of private illumination to her writing.

12

A few blocks away is Penn Station, where I arrived in New York for the first time, aged twenty. Emerging from the rush hour subway, this was exactly how I'd imagined the city to be. Vertigo-inducing towers, steam rising from a manhole cover. Everything porous and synaesthetic. I wanted to walk but was late to meet the friend I was staying with, and jumped into a cab. Broadway was so endless I was convinced the driver was bringing me somewhere else. On the leather seats, sweat prickling my neck, it felt like being inside someone else's creation: David Wojnarowicz's *Rimbaud*, Martin Scorsese's films and Nan Goldin's New York photos. A specific window of mid-1970s to early 1980s, which the city no longer resembles.

13

Wandering and watching were as much a part of Brennan's work as the act of writing itself. She possessed a unique ability to frame scenes into static moments and tip them carefully onto the page. This discreet surveillance formed the backbone of columns that celebrated the city, from its diners and parks to its architecture, where the Empire State was 'trying to be on nudging terms with every other building in the city'. Brennan as a non-native New Yorker saw the city through the same lens as a visitor. Each piece a small illumination of a life.

Although she may not have used the term about herself, Brennan was a *flâneuse* – navigating the city that gradually replaced Dublin in her affections. Brennan as wanderer, outsider, diviner of the streets that form an appendix to her work. She is one of Woolf's 'army of anonymous trampers', and the missing link between Woolf and writers like Vivian Gornick, whose walking of New York was an act of liberation from gendered expectations of her; or Rebecca Solnit, who makes the case for the right of women to walk alone, anywhere. Brennan's writing about walking, cities and loneliness echoes in Olivia Laing's *The Lonely City* and the Hopperesque scenes of isolated figures behind glass.

14

Brennan's columns are full of windows: looking in at the lives of others, or outwards from restaurant booths, watching the world. She rarely cooked, preferring to dine out alone. On late afternoons, she might take dinner at Marta's, or Le Steak de Paris on 49th Street (no longer to be found on my walk), or neatly perched at Schrafft's on Fifth Avenue near 46th Street. In one piece she explains that 'small, inexpensive restaurants are the home fires of New York City'. Another column, 'Balzac's Favorite Food', sees her sampling sardines on plain bread, a beloved dish of the French writer, who called the art of *flânerie* the 'gastronomy of the eye'.

15

I was in town another year, when the artist Marina Abramović was taking part in a public talk. As well as discussing her artistic process, she explained her love for the singularity of New York. The city, she said, had many virtues, but foremost was its unique energy, which nurtures and feeds artists. When asked where she thought it came from, Abramović explained that because New York is built of concrete, its energy seeps into everything, .

bouncing around between all those tall buildings. You can feel it, on every block, a kind of static hiss.

16

The sound of New York is its own song: car horns, the clatter of feet and the noise of construction. I have never walked more than a couple of blocks without encountering scaffolding or buildings veiled in green industrial nets. It has intensified in recent years, but was just as prevalent in Brennan's time. She lamented the 'ogre called Office Space that stalks the city and will not be appeased' and frequently railed against the 'white wreckers' dust'. She wrote of a city in flux, of few constants. Of views once familiar now obliterated as buildings climb, and the search for living space becomes a vertical one.

On my Maeve map, breadcrumbing my way through her addresses, there are ghost spaces: places long gone, offices transformed into condos, restaurants now corporate blocks; it's striking how many have been knocked down and rebuilt. Right around the corner, on 44th and Third, once stood Costello's, owned by Irish brothers Tim and Joe. It opened as a speakeasy in 1929 and Brennan was a committed regular. Today, there's more construction. Wide-necked men, dust-covered, shouting in New Jersey accents. I wince, not at their corrugated voices, but because pain makes me a poor *flâneuse*. I crave long city walks, but know my limitations. A familiar ache travels up my back. If only Costello's was still there, I could ease myself onto a bar stool and sip a Manhattan. One Irish writer trailing the ghost of another.

17

As it moves towards evening, I thread my way back down Broadway, guided by green street signs. The sun is a magnet, pulling all the colours of the day towards it. New York is a city of lurkers, which makes sense in a city where everyone and everything shares so little space. Brennan's columns captured that crammedness, of people sluicing along the sidewalks, the roads clogged with cars. I pass close to West 49th Street near Broadway, where she lived in a hotel and wrote that the area was one of 'shabby transience'. In a short story called 'A Snowy Night on West Forty-Ninth Street', she contradicts this, describing the view from her room in otherworldly terms: 'Broadway lights up to make a night-time empire out of the tumbledown, makeshift world ...' Elevation has a premium here: the best views are from a height. Rooftops peer out at all those rectangles of light, thrumming in offices and homes, down on the centipede sidewalks, far above the sour tang of garbage in summer.

18

My last stop – near the hotel – is the place I associate Maeve Brennan with more than any other. It's where she was arguably at her most content and productive. The brickwork of No. 5 East 10th Street is red and faded, the railings a web of iron curlicue. In the 1940s, Brennan wrote her longest work here, a novella called – aptly – *The Visitor*, which was published only after her death. Many of her other addresses are lost to the past, to the hurried movement of short residencies, but '5 East 10th Street' is written in her hand on the novella's manuscript. In

'Faraway Places Near Here', she moves through a series of apartments that were frequently stifling in hot, New York summers. Psychogeographers believe that something of the past lingers in every place. Outside on the front steps, I try to find a remnant of her, unsure if convening across the decades is an apt or foolhardy expectation. There were names on the various doorbells. If anyone had emerged, I'd have taken my chances and slipped past in a flash, taking the stairs up to her old apartment.

What's most striking about walking these Manhattan locations is their tight grouping. For all of New York's vastness – its sweeping avenues and vertiginous architecture – Brennan moved in small circumferences. The Algonquin, on West 44th, is just one street away from the old *New Yorker* office on West 45th. At the time of this walk, the magazine was based on Times Square. Standing outside its FedEx incarnation doesn't resurrect Maeve, typing away on the second floor, smoking endless cigarettes. There are many blanks in her own New York geography: several parts of the city she never visited, keeping to her own self-imposed perimeter. On this trip, I didn't make it out to Long Island, where she spent winters in East Hampton, and died in a nursing home there in 1993. Perhaps this is because my associations with Maeve are of Manhattan and Dublin; the grind of urbanity and the solitude of suburban roads.

19

When I came to write about this walk, retracing each step, I realise that it took place in 2013 – around the time that I started to write. Tentatively putting words and scenes on the page, unsure of where I wanted it to go. Finding Maeve Brennan was about trying to tentatively step into her world, but also to locate myself inside a literary framework. I wasn't assuming or expecting that she would light the path, but in some ways she did.

The route back to the hotel was illuminated by the sodium soak of streetlights, and maybe somewhere in the shadows was Maeve, complicated, smoking in a plume of spectral glamour, deciding which window to take a seat by that night.

Lucky Horseshoe

Kathleen Rooney

'Casino' comes from the Italian for 'little house' but the Horseshoe Casino in Hammond, Indiana, is neither especially small nor homey. A 400,000-square-foot gaming emporium built in the mid-1990s on the shore of Lake Michigan, it sits in the sands of Northwest Indiana, south of the Hammond Port Authority and north of Whihala Beach.

Rounding up, the Horseshoe lies about twenty-five miles from Chicago's far north side, the Edgewater neighbourhood that I reside in, and the Rogers Park one that my friend Eric does. Although Chicagoland gets considered a part of the Rust Belt, Eric's and my own occupations are white collar: we work as professors at DePaul University. The two of us met there as colleagues and bonded over our shared affinity for *flânerie*.

A dedicated saunterer, intuitively attuned to the moods of our city and an adept practitioner of on-foot phenomenology, Eric is one of the best people in the galaxy to take drifting walks with. He and I often use the Fridays we both have off to traverse Chicago like it's our job, meeting up at nine and not returning until five. I enjoy walking with him inherently because of his savvy as a peripatetic companion, but also because as a female walker – a *flâneuse*, I suppose – men stop harassing me when I walk with a man. The catcalls, honks and creepy followers I encounter alone disappear when Eric and I stroll together.

Summers, Eric and I both have off, allowing for even greater geographic and durational ambition than we display during the school year. That is why, in July 2017, Eric proposed that he and I walk from the Horseshoe to Chicago, an expedition that's not terribly vast in distance but looms legendarily in the local mind. If you tell someone from Illinois that you returned by foot to Chicago from Hammond, their eyebrows climb their scalps and their voices rise into an incredulous register before settling into a headshake and an expression of respect.

That summer, Eric had been getting into gambling. Such card games as poker and blackjack, he said, involved a measure of skill, thus rendering them superior to other casino offerings. So far, he'd only been practising by himself and playing online, but he was ready to test his aptitude in real life. Googling around, he'd found various hacks, including charts that helped the card player memorise likely hands, and tables of statistical probabilities for victory against the house.

But the best hack he'd uncovered, and the one that interested me – too risk-averse to ever be a gambler – was that the Horseshoe offers transportation from a variety of locations around Chicago directly to the casino door, free of charge. The most popular point of departure was Wentworth Avenue in the heart of Chinatown, not as far from our neighbourhood as Hammond itself, but still pretty far. But two miles south of my place, in the sub-neighbourhood of Uptown known alternately as New Chinatown and Little Saigon, was another shuttle hub.

From the Chicago Entertainment Tour, Inc. office roughly between a *banh mi* shop and the Furama Chinese restaurant, the shuttle departed hourly. To board, all you needed was to be over twenty-one. To get home, you showed your round-trip voucher, handed out by the driver when you disembarked, as well as your gambling receipt.

Only Eric would be gambling, but that was okay – I wouldn't need a receipt – because we'd get from the Horseshoe into the City of the Big Shoulders under our own steam, circumstances permitting. Eric, who has a higher tolerance for hazard than I, not only as a gambler but also as a *flâneur*, warned me that the route we'd have to take was dangerous: pedestrian-hostile, sidewalk-less, lined with overgrown medians, and rife with speeding vehicles. I despise cars. They're death machines. I haven't driven since 2010 because I detest being behind the wheel. This warning didn't please me, but I said I'd give it a shot.

On Thursday, 13 July – chosen for its forecast of overcast but not rainy skies to mitigate the eighty-five degree heat and humidity – we caught the 11 a.m. shuttle. When Eric and I rove the city proper, I often dress up. I like the aspect of *flânerie* by which the stroller, a bit dandyish, can play a charming role in someone else's scenery, lending style or colour to the panorama unfolding before those unnamed strangers. But that day, I wore jeans and boots, the better to brave the grit and glass of the unkempt asphalt, the shaggy shoulders.

The start of our escapade was sociologically interesting – so many people of so many different ages and races sat in the seats around us – but sedentary. The bus smelled of disinfectant and air conditioning, and the city streaked by on Lake Shore Drive through windows blurry with black mesh sun-screening. Nervousness crept electrically up my spine as the bus rolled up and onto the soaring Chicago Skyway. Built in 1958, the Skyway's name is vastly more romantic than its actuality: a 7.8-mile tollway connecting the Indiana Toll Road and the Dan Ryan Expressway on Chicago's South Side. But it really is in the sky, sort of, towering over the non-expressway streets below. We'd be walking down under its shadow eventually.

When the bus pulled us into the covered shuttle entrance, I tried to feel heartened by the huge word HORSESHOE on the nearby wall in lights, bright white bulbs filling in the letters in an old-timey Western font – all caps, like on a WANTED poster – even though we'd ridden east to get there.

Denotatively, 'to gamble' means to play games of chance for money; to bet. Metaphorically, 'to gamble' is to take a risky action in the hope of a desired result.

Our stakes in returning from the casino, as I calculated them, ranged from the not awfully costly outcome of having to summon a rideshare service to transport us home on four boring wheels – to the gory and incalculably high outcome of getting struck by a speeding truck and maimed or killed. The result we were hoping for, though, was simply to be able to walk all the way back into the city and get home from there by public transit.

First, though, Eric wanted to try his hand at the actual games of chance on offer. The casino reeked of cigarette smoke and the air freshener pumped in to drown out that reek. Preposterous crystal chandeliers protruded from the ceiling, casting light on the interlocking horseshoes adorning the carpet competing with the gleam of 3,000 slot machines and 250 video poker kiosks. The roulette wheels and the craps tables and the attendants inviting customers to play disheartened me.

While I people-watched – a depressing tableau consisting mostly of individuals losing money they couldn't afford not to have – Eric played $10-minimum blackjack and won $40 in ten minutes. An auspicious omen, he said, for our more important endeavour. He cashed in his chips and we left the Horseshoe to make the real gamble that would be our attempt to cross the state line.

And, at that point, we experienced the usual alteration of time and distance that only a long aimless amble can offer – the one I savour on every walk, no matter the area – a sensation like a shift in tense.

Emerging from the parking garage, we pass the Hammond Water Filtration Plant and innumerable train tracks, not all of them functional: blue chicory growing from between the ties, graffitied boxcars. Before we get onto the main thoroughfare of Indianapolis Boulevard that will take us beneath the Skyway, we meander through a residential neighbourhood with little beige houses covered in vinyl siding, awnings over the windows like lids over sleepy eyes.

In his 'Introduction to a Critique of Urban Geography' from 1955, Guy Debord writes that, whereas geography 'deals with the determinant action of general natural forces, such as soil composition or climactic conditions, on the economic struc-tures of a society, and thus on the corresponding conception that such a society can have of the world', psychogeography attempts to study the 'precise laws and specific effects of the geographical environment, whether consciously organized or not, on the emotions and behavior of individuals'.

Psychogeographically speaking, Lake County, Indiana, feels light years different than Cook County, Illinois – leery and vacant and less than friendly.

Debord adds that 'the charmingly vague adjective *psychogeo-graphical* can be applied to the findings arrived at by this type of investigation, to their influence on human feelings, and more generally to any situation or conduct that seems to reflect the same spirit of discovery'.

Our discoveries include mysterious ephemera. A bumper sticker on a guardrail we hop says in white font on a purple backdrop, 'Three things cannot be long hidden: the sun, the moon, and the truth', attributed to the Buddha. The truth is that Indianapolis Boulevard is an antagonistic place to walk; we don't see another single soul on foot. The car-centric strip of storefronts and restaurants features empty buildings with FOR RENT signs, billboards advertising FIREWORKS, and hamburger shops. The drivers and passengers of passing pickups and sedans eye us less with curiosity, more with suspicion. To walk here means to appear odd, potentially up to no good.

In *The Practice of Everyday Life*, Michel de Certeau explores how citizens can individualise mass culture, and he includes a chapter called 'Walking in the City' on how they can do so on foot, exploring their environment not from on high, but at street level.

He writes of New York City as seen from above, at the top of the now absent World Trade Center, from where 'the tallest letters in the world compose a gigantic rhetoric of excess', and asks, 'To what erotics of knowledge does the ecstasy of reading such a cosmos belong?' – contrasting the voyeuristic perspective of viewing the city from such a height with the eye-level perspective of the lowly pedestrian. He adds that their 'bodies follow the thicks and thins of an urban "text" they write without being able to read it'.

But as we approach the diciest part of the day's trip, the sunless strip beneath the Skyway, I beg to disagree with de Certeau. Psychogeography, with its attentiveness to how a given place makes the walker feel, gives the individual a way to read at least their own emotions and ideas about cities and the people in them. How they meet, how they interact, how they use their shared environment. Eric and I are reading our experience literally and figuratively, and we both agree that though we are barely two miles from the border, we miss Chicago.

We read the Horseshoe Casino sign, the most glamorous and appealing aspect of the gambling facility now far behind us, positioned to be a beacon for the traffic on I-90, evocative of Las Vegas with its mass and lights, a several-storey fountain-burst of yellow and red and orange arcing up from the earth, bedecked in bulbs and culminating in a giant H nestled in a horseshoe, open-side facing up for luck.

We hop another guardrail, this one with a bumper sticker quoting Ray Bradbury that I read aloud: 'You don't have to burn books to destroy a culture. Just get people to stop reading them.' We read a Unilever factory building advertising the soap manufactured within: 'Home of Dove, Caress, and Lever 2000'. The desolateness of a heavily built environment with no other walkers – not one – feels eerie. The inhospitability of the landscape mutely offers the answer as to why.

Under the Skyway, beneath the rush of I-90 West, black-eyed Susans look at us with impenetrable eyes and thistles grab our pantlegs from the unmown shoulder, like Indiana doesn't want us to leave. Like the hands of the damned in a horror movie holding us back. Or so it feels for a second to me. Eric seems fine, forging ahead as we proceed single file on the narrow sliver of walkable land.

We pass the 'Welcome to the City of Hammond/Mayor Thomas McDermott, Jr.' sign in reverse and have to turn back to photograph it. I pose with my parasol, grinning like some kind of demented tourist. I bet nobody else has this shot on their Instagram.

Cars and semis whip by as we walk on the median now in the middle of the streets beneath the Skyway, itself like the lid to a forgotten hell. The decrepit infrastructure with its peeling paint and bolted metal becomes our sky. The traffic is loud, very loud, loud as a river full of rapids and cataracts. It's hard to talk without shouting, which gives everything we say an angry edge whether we intend it or not. It's tense. I dislike it. I don't quite regret agreeing to this walk, but I'm not so much enjoying as I am enduring it.

Until we cross back into Chicago, that is, and feel instantly welcomed. Compass plants so named for the compass-like orientation of their leaves, line the roadside with their yellow petals. They, too, follow the sun, like we are in a sense, though the day is partly cloudy and we're going as much to the north as to the west.

We stand at the state line beneath the viaduct, a dusty pocket of urban wasteland made not to go to waste by a small tank put up by the American Legion, the plaque explains, to memorialise World War II. Beyond it rises a mural of the Blues Brothers, Chicago pride bursting beneath the boxcars above.

There are scarcely more pedestrians here than back on Indianapolis Boulevard, but there are a few and their presence transforms Ewing Avenue into friendly territory. The businesses, though not shiny or new by any means, seem to salute the passers-by, inviting them in. Route 66 Pizza, home to pasta, broasted chicken and sandwiches (do they 'broast' anything anywhere else than the Midwest?), appears amid auto body shops and billboards advertising McDonald's in Spanish, Vet's Bait and Tackle, Pucci's Restaurant and Pizzeria. We don't want to stop, but we're glad to see them. It feels better to have them and their clientele around than the place from which we've come.

In his short novel, *In the Café of Lost Youth*, Patrick Modiano writes of this intuitive method of psychogeography, 'I've always believed that certain places are like magnets and draw you towards them should you happen to walk within their radius …'

I admire how that book articulates the sense of inevitability and flow one can cultivate when walking in a city, 'a passivity and slowness that allow you to be softly penetrated by the spirit of the place'.

To be a psychogeographer means paying attention to the invisible, to the indefinable, why a certain street leaves you anxious and another content. Borders and boundaries. Places you stop and love and know you have to let go. Places that make you uneasy and you're relieved to leave behind. Eric and I are thrilled to be back in our beloved city. It took maybe an hour to get from the Horseshoe to here, but it felt like an aeon.

Ineffable are the reasons for our relief at being in East Side, Chicago's southern and easternmost neighbourhood. Ewing Avenue, the main drag, is obviously neglected, clearly the location of decades of disinvestment subsequent to the closure of the area's steel plants. Empty storefront after empty storefront line the avenue towards St George's Church. Yet East Side's vibe is far more benign than Hammond's.

Even its name as a neighbourhood, we say, is sort of magical. Because Chicago, snug against Lake Michigan, isn't popularly seen as having an east side, due to a body of water so big that if you didn't know what you were staring at, you'd think it was the sea. But in this part of town where almost nobody ends up by accident, the curve of the land into Indiana means there's so much more earth down here on this end of the lake that this network of streets exists for miles, a grid that doesn't occur at all on the far north side.

The only spot where the spirit of the place turns briefly malevolent – where I feel as though our gamble might not break our way – is in a sunken sideyard next to a rickety brick house. Inhabited or abandoned is anyone's guess, but at the property's edge stands a pale female mannequin, blonde-wigged, a child but life-sized and holding a difficult pose at the far edge of the vacant lot where maybe something was torn down and there used to be a garden. Eric and I both reach for our cameras – we've been snapping away this entire time – then decide against photographing her. We don't talk about why in that moment, but for me, it's because there's something chilling in her aspect. It's become a beautiful day, blue and sunny with a gentle breeze. Warm light illuminates the fake child completely, but her effect could not be colder. I don't even want her burned into my camera or to have a digital recollection of her. She's the kind of entity where maybe if you photographed her the image would possess a sinister power over you from then on. The neighbour-hood is run-down but still decently kempt in a lot of parts, so her ominous gaze is no mere function of her surroundings. It's all her. Who put her here and when did they do it? She looks in fair repair but also weather-beaten. Above all – why?

But as is the way with any drift worth its miles, we keep moving along and the atmosphere shifts again. We meet a *raspados* cart at 95th Street, where Eric buys a water from a Spanish-speaking lady wearing a hairnet and a red-checked apron, resisting the shaved ices with their cherry, coconut, pineapple, blue raspberry and piña colada syrups. We're almost to the region's most famous landmark, Calumet Fisheries, a no-frills seafood shack on the Calumet River, the set of industrialised canals that flow between South Chicago all the way to Gary.

Everything following the child mannequin is a cheery denouement. We did it. We crossed the state line. We are safely ensconced again in the city of our choice. We did not die, not even once. What luck!

The drawbridge above the channel rises. We wait, staring at the old steel bridges, and it's impossible not to time travel and think back to when this neighbourhood was a hub of industry – jobs for people, hopes for the future. Shipbuilding and iron-working. We drift north again past old-style signs advertising cold beer, a mural celebrating the 2016 World Series win for the

Cubs. Past God First Last and Always, Inc. whose sign tells us, 'God Loves You & Jesus Does Too!' – an unexpected message coming from a scrapyard with a bashed piano at the gate and a path leading in towards endless smashed cars.

Past a 1972 plaque memorialising 'the South Chicago residents who lost their lives in a commuter train accident on the Illinois Central Gulf Railroad'. Our own strategy today, because we are still about twenty miles south of where we need to be considered truly home, is to hop on a commuter train, the Metra Electric. But the remnants of that almost-half-century-ago tragedy doesn't faze us. We'll be okay. Like Eric at the blackjack table, we know we've won.

We slip by the various stops on the South Side up to Chicago's Loop, where we'll switch to the subway for the journey's final leg. Daydreaming through the green-tinted glass of the commuter train windows, we re-traverse at high speed the miles we covered by shuttle and foot.

To some people, *flânerie* – or drifting or psychogeography or whatever their preferred term – is an act of transgression or even subversion. But none of what Eric and I did felt so aggressive. It's been not so much a trespass as a creative misuse. The taking of an available but underused chance. Who else would ride the Horseshoe Casino shuttle to Hammond, then perversely walk back? Us, of course. We would. We did. Gambling costs money, but gambling on a walk is free, and for a few weird hours that day, so were we.

Depths of Field

Josephine Rowe

No people in this poem. As if it subsisted
by the very disappearance of places and people.

Czesław Miłosz, 'Reading the Japanese Poet Issa
(1762–1826)'

On the morning of his birthday, I send my loft-bound best friend a recording of a Yasunari Kawabata story. We were supposed to be meeting in Japan around this time, traipsing between mountain inns on the Nakasendo Trail. Instead, we remain a narratively tidy 10,000 miles apart, as the pandemic of 2020 moves from global anxiety to a lived reality.

In Australia there is a pervasive air of invulnerability; that we will be spared by our geographical remoteness (remote to where?), along with the national mythology of our exceptional grit. From my third-floor window in bayside Melbourne I mark the gradual differentiation in foliage across the season's shift, attempting to match birds to their calls.

In Toronto, the branches of the honey locust are beginning to show green outside Patrick's window, and Ontario has declared a state of emergency. At ground level, a family of emboldened racoons rummages in the overflowing dumpster behind the newly empty Value Village; prelude to a theme that will proliferate in months ahead – the greater non-human world creeping past the boundaries we have tried to impose upon it.

As the pandemic intensifies and as each of our cities turns inwards, in turn, we smuggle one another out of lockdown via FaceTime strolls through spaces urban and wild, trading dispatches from thawing city streets and jellyfish-strewn shorefronts, where frigid southerlies whip half my words away; audio snippets from boreal woods and eucalypt forests, punctuated by raucous cohorts of cockatoos and currawongs, or the high, lonesome tremolo of a loon.

We draw upon an ever-widening pantheon of beacons of solitude – the artwork of Agnes Martin, the rediscovered reel-to-reels of Connie Converse – and share passages from Robin Wall Kimmerer's *Gathering Moss*, which seems to speak to the heart of humankind's newly complicated relationship with the middle distance:

> We poor myopic humans, with neither the raptor's gift of long-distance acuity, nor the talents of a housefly for panoramic vision … With sophisticated technology, we strive to see what is beyond us, but are often blind to the myriad sparkling facets that lie so close at hand.

Much of our friendship – and some of our marriage, for the years we were married – has been lived at a distance. It started out that way, and after so many years perched at disparate latitudes, we've become adept at making do with whatever shared spaces we might find: a record, a film, or the sweet consonance of reading a book in step, or one on the heels of the other, travelling through the same landscapes and interiors, listening at the same doors, watching light enter the same rooms and weather define the same faces.

At proximity, the places we've sought out together often tend towards the liminal, the decommissioned or abandoned. Our first walk together was through an olive grove turned sanctuary for retired pianos – uprights and grands and pianolas and harpsichords slowly desiccating in the West Australian heat, tickled now and again by rain or visiting noise musicians, and otherwise home to snakes and tree frogs. Some of them still stately, still playable under peeling lacquer; others sifting quietly back to the earth, little more than an iron frame and a confusion of ivory keys scattered in the soil.

On the wall of Patrick's study, there is a blue hand-drawn map of a now-abandoned island in outport Newfoundland, where his mother was born. The map was made up as a souvenir for the island's 2016 Homecoming, the fiftieth anniversary of its depopulation.

Details its maker deemed map-worthy: that the island's name was changed to Bar Haven (rebranded, in a sense) from Barren Island in 1912, an anglicisation of the French Isle Sterile. That its church, St Francis Xavier, opened on 7 September 1919, and the population at the last census, before the 1966 Resettlement, was 243.

The map seems a composite of collective memory and more impartial, officially recorded topographies. An enlarged section shows the two main settlements, family names in sharpie caps with wavering lines connecting to where their homes once stood, along with the eponymic sea – and landmarks: Fish Rock, Black Duck Pond, Nannie's Garden, White Horse, The Yellow Marsh, Telegraph Cable from Judge's Cove, Otter Point Shoal.

The trail leading through the woods between settlements is unnamed, appearing as a clean unbroken line connecting Bar Haven to Western Cove, passing though Chapel Head, Pencil Hill, Salmon Cove Hill.

Ten years ago, Patrick took me to this island. Or, his father did, by motorboat, piloting us out from Swift Current. I write this and picture hand-built slipways, birch-boned and vertiginous, all through the province. And Ted, guiding the boat through the notoriously dense fog of Placentia Bay. His hands easy on the wheel, fingers splayed, missing thumb briefly obvious there. Crushed by rig machinery when he worked as a roustabout in his thirties. (After Resettlement, after the long foreshadowed collapse of the cod fishing industry, many islanders accustomed to offshore hitches found work in oil – fields and sands and offshore rigs.) Later, Patrick will tell me he's surprised his father gave the real story – no tricks with knives, no death matches with monstrous fish.

There was conflicting intel about the trail we'd be hiking that day – whether anyone had walked it in recent years, and to what extent nature might have reclaimed it. The old pass between the island's two settlements had been left to itself, ceded to moose and caribou, in the several decades since depopulation.

Probably, it still went right through, or no reason it wouldn't. Hard to get lost, anyway; no more than a few kilometres, and never too far from view or earshot of the ocean. Forty years ago, a small child could walk along, alone, without adult objection, to run errands to the cross-cove neighbours, or to earn a little extra money with some precocious industry. (That was Carmel, Patrick's mother, going from Bar Haven through the shaggy boreal woods to sell packets of seeds to those in Western Cove.)

There was talk of recutting this trail the following summer, when enough of the boys were home from Alberta, now that each of the hereto-abandoned settlements was seeing the stirrings of return; a seasonal influx of life, at least during the milder months of the year, simple summer cabins cropping up from the vacated plots of former family homes.

In 1961, at age eleven, Carmel moved with her family to mainland Newfoundland. They were among the first in a five-year drive that would see the island's entire population relocated, along with tens of thousands of others throughout the province under the edict of government Resettlement programmes during the 1950s to 1970s. The highly controversial programmes were an economic bid to centralise and modernise the scattered outport communities, whose residents numbered around 30,000, and whose livelihoods were hitched to a vulnerable fishing industry.

*   *   *

The scent comes back to me sometimes. If I try I can summon it, nearly as well as I can the dry, peppery scent of the Australian bush, when I've been away too long. Or elements of it might blindside me; the Avalon Peninsula looming up resinous and lush from a hint of sharp green sap, or from a stray trace of smoke. Spruce, first and foremost, topmost. And underneath that, salt mist and wood smoke, and the sweetish smell of boat fuel on wet air.

*   *   *

The journey from Swift Current takes around forty-five minutes over fourteen nautical miles. Across this same distance, the houses of Bar Haven and neighbouring island communities were floated on rafts fashioned from birch logs and oil drums, and towed to mainland Newfoundland by any available watercraft.

In Atlantic Canada, this image – of the two-storey weatherboard cast adrift on open water, or being hauled by cables across the ice – is ubiquitous, a household print framed and foxed on every other living room wall, or pressed between the plastic leaves of family photo albums, or slipping from shoeboxes of ephemera at rummage sales. Many of the rafts do not look altogether seaworthy; houses must surely have tipped off, or simply fallen through like an animal over a thatched pit trap, sinking deep to the bed of the Bay. But Ted can only remember that happening once.

The only building left standing on the island was the church, comparatively grand for such a small parish, built of brick and thus immoveable. The church remained, along with headstones in the graveyard, the concrete and stone substructures from which the humbler wooden houses had been lifted, the wooden jetties left to weather and salt, gnawed by sea, the paths left to grow over, to wander off into animal tracks.

Some years after depopulation, the church was set alight by arsonists – known or unknown, depending on whom you ask – and left to topple in on itself. Everybody says the priest was cosy with the Brooklyn mafia. Everybody says, 'Well, that's just what people say …'

When I ask what Patrick remembers, he says, 'All the same things as you.' Which proves to be not quite true – although we have revisited this walk so many times in the past decade that there is a carbonising of certain recollections, others are individually fixed in a sort of double exposure.

What holds common, coheres: Ted drops us at the jetty with our daypacks and we start out on the northern side of the sandbar, for which the island is now named. We kick through long grass in borrowed Baffins, overlarge, our clumsy boot-tips seeking out the stone doorstep of the house where Carmel was born. The house itself no longer stands. Or at least, not here; it was towed across the Bay with all the others and sold on, for fifty dollars, and for all we know may still be providing shelter wherever it was brought aground.

We do not find the doorstep. We find instead the foundations and crumbling concrete vats from the fish processing plant that Carmel's family ran. She and her siblings ate lobster in their school sandwiches because there was not yet a market for it. They went around in a little gang of kids, crushed tin cans strapped under their shoes. There was a bolshy rhyming chant they had, which she once recited for us, hazy now – I remember the cadence but not the exact words. They were something about not giving a damn, or a fig, or a pin. I remember, more clearly, her laugh, restored to childhood's brass in that moment.

On the other side of the harbour, a cluster of new cabins in varying states of completion and ingenuity. The humblest and possibly the oldest belongs to Carmel's brother, Bernard, a master twineman and among the first to return. His cabin is little more than a one-room boathouse built of chip and weatherboard, perched at the end of a jetty. A simple bench indoors, a grille for cooking hung from a nail on the outer wall.

Sometime during the 1990s, former islanders cottoned on that while Resettlement compensation had been paid out, the land had never been officially transferred away from the title holders; they, or their families, still had a claim to the plots where their houses had once stood. Since then, those forced to leave as children have been trickling back, with their children, and have set to building anew.

What do we carry, between us: notebooks and pens, not enough water and not enough snacks of no memorable sort other than the vividly recalled peanut butter sandwiches, vivid because we ate them last, when famished. A bottle of beer ...

No, Patrick tells me, we didn't do that. Definitely can't see us drinking a warm beer.

... a bottle of beer that maybe we cooled in a stream up there somewhere? I have a vague recollection of us cooling beer in a stream.

That's a romantic idea, but I'm pretty sure that didn't happen. Knowing us, we probably took a flask of something. Whisky.

Moving on: we carry a hip flask of whisky and something else to drink that isn't cold enough. Possibly some kind of esoteric soda bought by the pallet at Costco.

We find our way to the cemetery, just the two of us, noting evidence of recent maintenance by an unknown hand, fresh white paint on neatened pickets that border the graves ...

Or: We do not find our own way to the cemetery. We find it later, with Emmet.

Fine. Emmet shows us there.

There he is, in an orange boiler suit on the other side of the harbour, hammering at a deck. Then waving hugely. Calling out to us as we approach – before we can ask for bearings, before we can offer our names – to come in for a mug-up.

They call it a cabin, Emmet and his wife, Donna; lofty ceilings and the new blonde boards making for honeyed light. We're sat at their table, mugged-up filter coffee and blueberry pancakes fresh from the hotplate. So, you're Carmel Farrell's boy? No strangers here.

Their windowsills are lined with findings, a kind of egalitarian reliquary. The largesse of children who skin-dive the harbour, scrabbling at the ocean floor like otters and surfacing with coloured glass bottles tossed into the sea half a century before.

More carefully stowed, nested in cotton wool, are the objects unearthed by Donna's own hands, salvaged from the ashy soil beneath the ruined church: a string of rosary beads, a vase, a salt shaker. Christ without the crucifix, the wood burned away in the same fire that destroyed the church. Figure of the heat-warped saviour held in the silt for forty years. Anointing bottles, charred part of a railing, shards of stained glass – no one artefact treated as more precious than the others, none held for any longer in her hands as she offers them to ours.

Her husband has his own rituals of preservation, talking us through a small archive of photographs, photocopies of photographs. The cavernous interior of the once-glorious church; a woman whose face is always scratched out, always by her own hand. Portraits of young men chiacking on whaling boats, manning a harpoon, posing before the immense penis of a humpback.

Emmet walks us as far as the cemetery, where he's been propping up the old headstones that climb the steep hillside, repairing the neat white fences around the graves. He expounds upon the perfunctory details of headstones – spellings of family names varying down the years, through dearth of literacy – annotating the denouements of those interred: tuberculosis, typhoid, childbirth, the five-year-old girl who fell from a kitchen chair while holding a sharpened pencil which pierced her eye. The island was iced in for the winter and there was nothing, or not enough, that could be done for her.

*　*　*

'Tuckamore' is the name given to evergreen trees – particularly spruce – that grow tangled and bent almost sideways, crouched low to the earth in an effort to withstand the constant force of coastal winds. Their roots spread out over the earth, clinging with gnarly tenacity. It is difficult to find literary reference to this distinctive Newfoundland growth formation that does not draw a line, overt or oblique, between the resilience of these trees and that of the people.

*　*　*

From the cemetery, we set off on the trail through the woods, visible enough after all, if now and again overwritten or divaricated by the desire lines of other creatures. Hoof and paw and claw prints in the mud of the path, veering off into the underbrush. We are contradictorily consoled by such depictions of nature's propensity to recoup, reclaim from our kind; what we tend to call 'rewilding', when there is human intent behind it. In this instance, however, the natural order of repossession has nothing to do with us. Human presence, human intent, is once again a flickering, transient thing here.

The air chirrs with bird and frog and insect talk, a fugue of biophonic transmissions.

Isle Sterile; a certain ring to it. Though the French must have stopped by in winter.

Whatever it was called before – by the Beothuk, and their forebears, who would likely have frequented such places as migratory hunting and fishing grounds – is lost. There are scant records, wordlists containing a few hundred Beothuk translations: those for capelin, bakeapples, dogberries, deer – all as plenteous now as then, though the people who spoke these words, bestowed these names – *shamook*, *abidemasheek*, *menome*, *osweet* – are themselves gone.

We make our way up an incline so gradual we barely notice. Or in any case, will afterwards barely recall. Again and again – in recollection as in life – we arrive at the hill-top meadow, where the trail is swallowed whole. Here we wade across the bawn of waist-high grass, bewildered by intermittent satellites of trampled grass; large round flattened patches, mysterious as crop circles and cosy as childhood cubbies. At last it clicks: moose nests. Here is where the big ungulates have deemed fit to sleep, out in the open, with their great shaggy muzzles turned towards the sea – untroubled by the chief predator of their mainland cousins, who shipped off long before their own lifetimes.

Where have they gotten to, these moose? To my mind they are crepuscular animals – retroreflective eyes irradiant as they manifest from roadside woods, crashing on spectacularly or standing stock-still at the verge while you slow the car to a crawl and plead, Don't bolt Don't bolt Don't bolt, silently or out loud. Do they bed down in the meadow by day, or night, or both? Perhaps they're off browsing the woods, tearing strips off the aspen or dredging up pondweed, or have they heard us coming and just now loped off for forest cover? And by what route?

There is no obvious way out of the meadow. No clear remnant of human desire lines. Or, not to our eyes, not now. Maybe earlier light would have shown us, but the damp air already has the indigo tint of nightfall. Here and there are shadowy alcoves, antechambers between the trees that might be openings to somewhere, elsewhere. We double over, burrow through bracken, over moss-furred rocks, wet our feet this side and that of a stream in an attempt to follow its logic; it can only flow in one direction, after all. One of us – him, I think – tweaking an ankle. As in any enchanted place, each promising path out disintegrates, closes in on itself after a short way, steadily blurs into impassable forest, or, after much meander, circles back in on the meadow to deposit us at yet another vantage, to stumble again through the waist-high grass amidst the nests of absent moose.

The light is going, together with the battery on Patrick's phone, the GPS showing us that we are only halfway. The Newfoundland damp creeping through the layers of our clothing, making itself right at home in our bones. But we are two kinds of stubborn – a child could do it, after all – so on it goes. Each of us beating our own way through the bracken along paths unknown to the other, merging now and then in the telling, diverging, but always meeting in the pasture with the darkness bending down. We return to this story, to the telling of it. Arriving each time from a new angle, crashing through a different copse of trees. The tangling and the getting lost become as much a shared home as any bricks and mortar.

At last the gloaming spills in and our pride dissolves, becomes secondary to good sense, and to good manners, because by now there are people, his people, turning lights on in a cabin on Western Cove, wondering about just when the two of us are going to emerge from the backwoods.

Anticlimax, almost beside the point: from the elevation of the meadow we discover that this island off an island, out of time and socked in by fog, has remarkable reception. If the GPS cannot show us where this undocumented trail reopens, we can at least send co-ordinates to Ted, then scrabble down the least precarious cliffside scree, through what is or isn't tuckamore, to wait at the nearest accessible cove. Listening for the motor to announce itself above the breakers, peering through the fog to watch the boat materialise in the last of the light. The air very blue now, inky, and the water grey-black and silver, we wade out into the shallows, the icy Atlantic sloshing over the tops of whoever's boots these are.

There are fixtures, footholds, holdfasts that we cling to, rely on to furnish a serviceable ending. The rope ladder is a good one; it stays always just where it is, secured to the side of the boat. Solid enough that when your foot finds the lowest rung the boat heaves to with your weight.

We are very young, I wrote then, at twenty-five, in a blunt blue pencil rummaged from his grandfather's stationery box. *We are not sure if the important things have happened to us yet.*

The important things. Of course some of them had. Others were waiting just out of frame, or remain so. Still, writing those words, I must have recognised that this was one of them, or would become as much; this getting lost, being reminded of our smallness even in so small a space (remote to where, to whom?).

Years later, there remains something urgent, consequential in the unseen second half, the unwalked mile of trail still concealed in woods. A longing to see beyond the known, in the way we crane our necks to peer around the corners of certain films, photographs.

In the boat, we lean against each other, too exhausted and sheepish to speak, looking starboard to the coastline and scanning the dark, now-solid mass of forest above for clues to another way we might have taken.

Out of My Cage

Kamila Shamsie

I know this street. I've known it all my life – or close enough for that statement to feel true. My parents, sister and I moved into a house on this street when I was seven years old, and though I moved away to London a while ago it's still a place to which I attach the word 'home', and to which I return every winter. So, I know this street. How could I not?

And yet, I don't know this street at all. The thought comes to me one winter day when I put on my walking shoes and, in the company of my sister, Saman, walk out of the gate and onto the street. I haven't gone more than a few paces before a feeling of strangeness, almost of wrongness, comes over me. I am walking down the street on which I've lived since I was seven years old – for the first time.

It isn't a walking city, Karachi, city of my birth and upbringing. If you want to walk, as I often do, you get into a car and drive to a park which has a walking track looping around it – the one which I frequent has a one-kilometre track which means

I seldom walk more than three or four kilometres before stopping from the monotony of walking in circles. But while there are several such parks within a few minutes drive of where I live, the city streets themselves have always felt inhospitable, out of bounds. This changed when lockdown in 2020 shut the parks, and far away in London I sat amazed at the messages from Saman and my parents saying, 'We went for a walk on our street.' It seemed thrillingly transgressive. So, now I'm in Karachi and though the parks have long since reopened, I want to walk down the street, and beyond it to the sea less than three kilometres from our house.

Saman and I set off together. The temperature is in the mid-twenties, which is winter weather for a Karachi afternoon. There's barely a cloud in the sky. I have only ever seen the houses on our street from a car window, and it hasn't previously occurred to me that driving allows you to glance whereas walking allows you to *look*. So I look at the houses of my neighbours. There isn't a great deal to see, since high boundary walls impede most of your view. But I notice for the first time which of the houses have flowerpots and shrubs outside the boundary walls, and which don't. A few days earlier, a friend in California sent me pictures of her aloe vera plant and I marvelled at the spikes growing between the fleshy leaves, the flowers at the tip of them. Now I see that a neighbour across the street has exactly such a flowering aloe in red pots outside his house. I stop to look at the plant and a cat walks past. It's one of the cats that wanders in and out of our garden and I imagine – or I notice – that it looks at me strangely, as if to wonder what I'm doing out of my cage.

We walk further. Someone important – a diplomat, perhaps? – lives on the street and I've often noticed the guards in camouflage uniform stationed outside one particular house. What I haven't previously noticed is the guards' use of the electricity wire that loops low down outside the house as a clothes line. There is a camouflage uniform hanging on it. I try not to think about the wisdom of hanging wet clothes on an electricity wire.

Because this isn't a city for walkers, there is often no proper pavement, and certainly no walk signals. Saman and I dash across a three-lane boulevard – luckily the traffic is light – and a few minutes later we're waving hello to Juni and Zehra, another pair of sisters, who we've known since childhood. Juni and I live in London, Zehra and my sister in Karachi. Every summer we meet in London, and sometimes further afield – the Left Bank in Paris, the ruins of Kenilworth. We always break into pairs as we walk – Zehra and I are 'fast walkers', Juni and Saman 'slow walkers'. We use these terms to lightly taunt each other – we fast walkers are told we don't stop to pay attention to things that matter; in turn we tell the slow walkers that they dawdle through life.

In any group of four friends, of course, there's always more than one way of slicing things. Zehra and my sister are the locals who have walked together to the beach many times since the parks closed; for Juni and I, this walk is something new and, like a pair of tourists, we keep pointing out sights along the way: the beautiful tree with yellow flowers hanging over a boundary wall, the appealing seating arrangement outside someone's house that offers weary travellers shade and rest, the blanket lodged into the cleft of a tree. And then, mysteriously on the side of the road, there's a steel water-cooler, with a protective cage around it, too heavy to move, and an opening in the cage that allows you to turn on the taps and fill a container or the cupped palms of your hands. It's a strange mixture of hospitality and suspicion that is perfectly suited to this city – be generous, it says, but don't be foolishly idealistic about human character.

We are still in a residential neighbourhood and the streets are largely empty, but every so often cars or bicycles or pedestrians move past us. The cyclists and pedestrians are all men – as are almost all the drivers of the cars. No one bothers us. We are middle-aged, I realise; it's a strange shock to attach that word to myself in the city of my childhood. In our younger days, we wouldn't have managed this walk without men slowing down their cars to drive alongside us, trying to engage us in conversation, or staring at us as we walked past. But now we are almost invisible to them. It's a relief, but there lurks some irritation beneath.

We are invisible, also, to the street dogs. They roam all around the neighbourhoods of Karachi, lean-framed with elegant muzzles, their coats different combinations of dun and white. Zehra calls our attention to how proud they look, how noble, and I find myself noticing them in a way that I never have before. She's right – whether they're moving in packs or singly there's a jauntiness to their step, a disdain for humans and traffic. They show no sign of wanting anything from us – not food, not affection, not attention. What must they think of domestic dogs? I ask, and Zehra says they must pity them for their neediness, their subservience. I love dogs, but I've never thought of the nature of Karachi's street dogs before; it's the walking, I know, that makes this possible – here we are, dogs and humans, legs moving us forward along the same roads. 'Hello!' Zehra says to the dogs that pass by, 'Hello, uncle!' They pad by, light on their feet, uncaring.

A few weeks later we will all think of these dogs with sorrow. A friend will lose her two puppies to poisoned meat that is scattered through the streets to kill 'strays' – a bird picks up the poisoned meat and drops it in my friend's garden, where her two Labradors find it. We've all grown up with these horror stories: from time to time some municipal body, prompted by complaints from citizens, decides it's time to cull the street dogs. There is no warning, no notification. But birds start to fall out of the sky after swooping down onto poisoned meat, and pet dogs die horribly after eating what was meant for their poor cousins. But all this is still unimagined and unimaginable as we walk towards the sea, ignored by the almost-prancing dogs.

Saman points out that Juni and I, despite living in the same city, haven't seen each other for over a year. This seems impossible, but it's true. We have a friendship as a foursome, and somehow it rarely occurs to Juni and me to meet when the other two aren't around. A few minutes after my sister makes her comment, Juni and I start walking side by side, leaving the other two behind. 'You've become a fast walker,' I say to Juni. We turn to wait for the other two to catch up so I can tell Zehra she has joined the ranks of the slow walkers. 'No, no,' says Zehra. 'I've been watching you. You slowed down, Juni sped up. And I slowed down and Saman sped up. We've all adjusted for each other.'

We are all delighted by this, as if it proves something about a give and take at the heart of our friendships. There are such things as walking friendships, of course. Which is to say, there are people with whom you'd happily set off across a city or up a mountain or through fields and forests – and then there are people with whom you simply never raise such a possibility. For all our jokes about dividing into slow walkers and fast walkers, we know how fortunate we are that all four of us walk together so well – we can walk as a foursome or in pairs and, crucially for a walking group, are content for one to go ahead or fall behind, wandering away from conversation. Keeping pace – either conversationally or more literally – is not a necessary part of a walking friendship. Someone falls behind, someone's attention drifts away – everyone else carries on, and when you're ready to rejoin the pack, there's always space to do so.

My own thoughts drift as we approach the sea. From my childhood through adolescence, my best friend lived in one of the blocks of flats that faces the sea, and in the last few months I've been working on a novel, set in the 1980s, in which I've made that block of flats the home of one of my fictional characters. Working on the novel has made me recall with nostalgia the time I spent in the flat while also recasting it as space in which I bring wholly imagined characters to life – it's a strange feeling now to be so close to a place that has occupied the space between memory and imagination in my mind for the last year or so. But it's so changed – the newly built flats of the eighties now battered and rusted by the corrosively salty air coming off the sea; and also, oddly, the building feels more stunted.

The blocks of flats and the trees planted in street-dividers hide our view of the sea until we are almost upon it. In my memory the smell of the sea comes at you long before the sight of it, but my memory is wrong – or perhaps based on some day where the wind blows differently. We are at one moment walking alongside high walls – trying not to stare at the man with gold chains around his neck and beautiful black ringlets of hair falling to his shoulders, who is striding with a bottle of Coke in his hand as though in an ad that suggests a kind of macho cool comes to those who drink the right carbonated product – and the next moment we are out on the street that runs parallel to the beach.

This is the most perilous part of our journey. It's a busy street – cars, vans and motorcycles zipping in both directions – and we stand for a while, watching them go past without any sign of let-up, until impatience propels us forward and we dart between the speeding vehicles to reach the low sea wall. The tide is far out and the sand stretches in front of us a long way, dark-grey. I imagine the surface of the moon might look like this. We make our way along the sand towards the blue-grey water. This isn't a swimming beach – you have to drive an hour or so from here to reach the clearer waters where you'd want to immerse yourself – but the sea still pulls everyone to it. There are hundreds of people here – Clifton Beach, as this has been known since colonial times, is Karachi's most popular spot – and all have trekked across the long stretch of sand towards the water's edge where some men push ice-cream carts and others offer rides in dune buggies and boys run up and down with roses that

they'll try to sell to any couple who look as though they're here
for a romantic outing.

One man in particular catches my attention. He's facing the
sea, seemingly oblivious to all around him. He's wearing a
close-fitting cap with blue and white geometric designs on it,
his face framed by a short beard, two silver bangles on his wrist.
He could be any age from thirty-five to fifty-five. He's holding
a square piece of cardboard with a rough diagram of a palm on

it. SHOW HAND is written along one side of the cardboard, with a less abrupt version of the message written in Urdu along the other. He's a palm-reader, but it feels as though it would be intrusive to thrust a palm in front of him when all he clearly wants is to stand and watch the waves.

Anyway, the sun is setting now, and women walking in the dark is a very different thing to women walking in sunlight. We make our way back through streets that already, on return, feel familiar in a way that they haven't ever felt familiar before. But that's another walking story.

Shore

Cynan Jones

I look again at the Tide Tables. This year's is barely thumbed. The note with it, from my wife, not this Christmas nearly on us, but the one before, tucked inside its cover. *Use your time.* There's a kiss, and her initial.

When I look down the tide columns, I don't see numbers, I see a particular beach.

I know which of the 'marker' rocks will be uncovered; how deep the retained water in the pools will be.

I also know, after all this time, I will not be wholly right.

* * *

My feet crunch and slip. It's an awkward beach. A west-facing stretch, some two miles long, strewn north-eastward from the village a short way from where I live.

Since the sea defences were improved in front of the town to the south, the shore here has taken the hit. The stones are cast petulantly around, so it's difficult to walk with rhythm. Particularly since my knee. I have to steppingstone.

When I was doing this regularly, the choice of where to put my feet was often all I thought about, one stone after the other, until I got to the net. I'll have to relearn that.

I've not put the nets out since my daughter was born. I've kayaked and brought back mackerel, but the net has been too much. She's nearly three.

I imagine bringing her home a fish. A great big fish she won't believe. Before another year is out.

*   *   *

Up the beach I can see the deep undercuts in the clay. Sporadically, faces have given in and slumped onto the stones. It seems the whole brim of the land has slackened and come forward.

A group of gulls hang almost motionlessly high above, printed on the pale sheet of sky.

Months, one after the other, of clear precise numbers.
January, February, on to December again, with no biro marks
at all. Until yesterday, one dot.

Yesterday I laid the net near the peninsula, beyond which the
shore broaches away, turns sandier, and is flanked by low flat
fields.

Off that peninsula, the beach is monumented with great
chunks of grey rock, like daises that have come off the cliff.

It feels to me this marks the point of the bay where south
meets north. A point that also separates two phases of my life.

I grew up, the first eleven years, just north of the peninsula.
My grandparents had farmland there that went right to the sea.

Then we moved six or so miles south, to the place I still am
now, a short way from this beach.

Several times, I've walked from home to the cliffs and along
the shore to the village I first lived in, the second village 'up'.

When I do, I pass the first village, where my mother went to
little school, the pitch of my teenage football team; then the
lime kilns – once my private castle, signs now, Keep Out;
and onto land that used to be my grandparents'. Always, I
thought then.

I go up the beaches – I had a pale blue dumper-truck toy –
over the short rattling bridge – my brother more confused
than I at the tiny brook trout on his line, the rainbow of it
gone by the time we got it home – to the small estate.

I stand at the entrance of the estate. And then I chicken out. I
don't go to the childhood bungalow, but, each time, I feel the
crystally pebbledash come off the wall under my hand.

*   *   *

Water runnelling off the land has cut deep channels into the
slid clay. From out at sea it makes this section of the cliff look
like a set of teeth.

The impression, from distance, is defiance. Bared. Jaw set
against the ocean.

In front of the section, the remains of a twelfth-century fish
trap run in a curve, like a bite mark. A geometric arc of
heavy rocks.

Way out, beyond the eye, are other walls, sunk. Walls. Glacial
moraines. Which would you prefer?

Some twenty miles north, when powerful storms carry the
sand off the beach, the stumps of petrified trees can be
uncovered. Pine, alder, birch, oak. The preserved wattle of a
Bronze Age walkway built to traverse sodden ground. The
things they've found. The skeleton of an aurochs. The
footprint of a four-year-old.

Off the shore I'm on now, the remnants of an Ice Age
causeway. One of seven that became the ways, or *sarnau*, to a
fertile land, that lay, it is certain, below the level of the sea.

I imagine farmers at low tide cart out beyond a great
embankment to harvest seaweed for their crops; ditches drain
salt water from the fields; the disciplined rank that man the
sluices. And then the lip of the world curl up.

Land for thousands of years before the dyke, and until the
dyke was breached, blame shifting with the ages. A priestess
careless of a fairy well; a noblewoman swept up by a king;
a soldier.

How that must have felt. Miles away at court. To hear the
far-distant crack of waves against the dyke; the throb of the
storm. The watch-candle guttering. Awake suddenly and sick
and drunk, but lucid with the knowledge your men are too
well drilled to close the gates without your orders.

Your futile ride into the throat of the storm. The wall of ocean.

We have a Shoreline Management Plan here that sets out policies to address the hundred years ahead of rising sea levels and advanced erosion. The language that describes the options for each coastal settlement is military: Hold the line; Advance the line; Managed retreat; No active intervention.

I grew up believing that on quiet nights I might hear the kingdom's drowned bell ring under the water.

*　　*　　*

There's a shifting off-protein stink in the air and I scan around for the dogfish. I don't even have to look to know the softer skin under its gullet is cut. Fishermen do this. Perhaps to retrieve their lures or perhaps because they just don't want to catch them. Or perhaps they're thrown from the nets of the boats that have filled the horizon recently in a line that looks like festive lights.

I haven't been conscious of a breeze particularly, but when I spot the twisted fish, the inevitable gape in its neck, it's behind me. The wind has changed since yesterday. Yesterday the stink hit me before I got to it.

I caught dogfish once. Plurally. I made the mistake of putting shore pots out, just a little way from where I lay the net.

The dogfish came in, drawn by the smell of the pot bait, and hit the net. They were all in the very base of the mesh, having nosed their way along the shore bed, truly like dogs.

There was also a smooth-hound in the net, even more properly sharklike than the dogfish; unlike them, though, it was very clearly dead.

I got the dogfish out. Their upper skin, softly leatherish when I ran my hand down their backs, sandpapered layers off me when they wrapped in my grip. Their bodies had the dense pulsing flexibility of snakes. Some shot white mess from their vents. They were all alive and they all went back into the water, leaving my hold slowly and S-ing down to the seabed, as if to take stock.

But the smooth-hound's eyes were closed. It gave the huge dead fish an agony. I felt terrible. When I held it up, it was as long as I was, and I was bereft. I'd not caught anything I didn't want before.

Even so, I coiled it into the large council recycling bag I had with me, and – because I lived with her at the time – put it in my mother's fridge.

The next morning there was a note on the fridge: Shark Out! I found that funny.

My intention was to fillet the long loins that run from behind the head to where the tail becomes too thin to eat. I was going to cut them up and cook them in milk.

A friend was round to help me get things into the attic. He was passing boxes through the hatch.

When I called down to put the kettle on, he opened the fridge for the milk.

The smell hit me even through the bungalow ceiling.

I cannot detach the initial force of the smell from the sound my friend made right at that moment. Then I heard the door crash open, and retching, muted through the gable wall.

I had nowhere to go. The smell was so loud I could barely think. My friend was gagging now and in the horror of it I started to laugh. I had to go through the hatch and *into* the smell.

I reached into the fridge.

The shark had sweated something and sat ringed in some off-grey liquid in the bag. It felt like the shark itself was dripping. Out. I ran with it, praying the bag wouldn't leak, tipped it onto the ground, the smell, the ammonial thud of the shark.

I lifted it by the tail. Just wanted to get it gone. But it had stiffened. It uncoiled only into a five-foot-long boomerang, face bent like it was trying to grin back up at me.

I ran. Again. Out. Through the gate. Then with a sort of hammer-throw sent the carcass up and away into the scrub.

For a horrible moment it hung in a tree. Then it plunged into the bramble.

For weeks I imagined some poor dog walker. Their face when their dog wandered out of the Common with a dead shark in its jaws.

* * *

The sound of runnel water now has changed. The tap-left-on sound through soft clay now a clatter-down hard stone. A bright mist of waterfalls.

I've reached the point where the cliff has been taken back to rock. The juncture sudden. One moment clay, which looks combative and attritional; then impassive, stratic blocks.

The *peep* of an oystercatcher; *strike* of a pipit; occasionally the *craw* of choughs tumbling on the thermals.

Last Christmas, from up there on the path high above, I saw a bolt of colour blur across the exposed shore. Watched the livid dot of the kingfisher fish along the pools, as if it set pace with me, for half an hour, before it flew away in a straight quick flight.

Even as I watched I knew it was something I would never see again.

In the corner of my eye a piece fractures from the cliff and scimitars off. Peregrine.

I only ever see them come off the rock section, as if they are a product of it.

Over the clay, ochre and grey, is a kestrel sometimes, hung, then slipping on the air.

When I look back down the beach, at the clay wall, I see a distraught section of fence suspended mid-air.

Jackdaws perch and lift, perch and lift, sound out a subdued clang as a dislodged fencepost dips and strikes a fallen trough.

* * *

I do not see the fish until I'm right over it. A grey mullet as long as my arm, lain tangled in a shallow pool at the far end of the net.

My heart knocks. Daughter's wide eyes. Tufts of fennel that have defied the frost. The fish's scales bigger than her fingernails.

I should free the rope from the anchor stones. Take the net towards the beach, deal with the knot of it there. Free the fish without the pressure of the tide.

Then the fish flicks powerfully and I see it gape.

* * *

I try to work quickly. The fish seems to dull as I do. I lift, loop
the net from its fins, gills, tail, mouth. Feel again an over-
awareness, a process I've lost. Feet finding the stone ahead;
fingers finding loops themselves.

Thinking too hard about the puzzle. The pressure of the fish
alive. And at the front of my mind, the incoming water. A fizz
each time it drags across a nearby pad of ragwormed sand,
tongues into the pool in which I try to keep the mullet rested.

My feet get wet.

Every time I think the fish is gone, it bleats silently.

Come on, I'm saying. Come on.

*   *   *

By the time the fish is loose, the tide is in around my knees.

Bent, bare-armed, I hold the fish into the waves. For a
moment before I push it down, I see my hand around its foiled
back, the concentration, her small hands crimp a silver
cooking parcel. Then it's in the water. I feel it gulp beneath the
surface. As I watch the bright lace of waterfalls, the beach
narrow south. To the north, the broaching shore.

It's settled, I tell myself. The sea will not get up.

No way to bring the net out now.

The beach disappearing. Think: I'll have to come just after dawn. To meet the ebb. Tomorrow.

Leave the net. It will *make* you walk. The habit will come back.

There's still some year left.

Then the fish bucks once. It seems to fill with sudden strength, and I let it go.

Lot's Wife, and Some Reflections on Walking at Night

Nicholas Shakespeare

A walk doesn't have to take long to be meaningful. For the Czech artist Helga Hošková-Weissová, at the age of fifteen, it was the length of a ramp. Yet hers was the ultimate walk that transcends all walks, a journey from the dark to the light.

A German officer stood at the head of the ramp directing people right and left. 'I don't remember his face, only his gloves, but his face is not important. The important thing was his finger, because with his finger he pointed right, left, right, left.' As she put one hesitant foot towards him, then another, for whatever reason the man lifted his finger and snarled at her, '*Rechts!*'

Helga told me this in the same Prague apartment where she had grown up, seventy years later. 'I am often asked if this was Josef Mengele. Probably it was.'

Like no other action, to walk is to affirm that you are alive on this earth. If a single image encapsulates Tel Aviv, a city where Jews really could be themselves for the first time, it is feet. Bare. In flip-flops. In orange trainers. In green high heels. In office slip-ons. But no longer the feet of the Wandering Jew, in flight and pursued since the time of Abraham. An English traveller to Tel Aviv, Dorothy Kahn, made this lovely observation, that once you have caught the music in the freedom of these feet – jogging, playing beach tennis, pedalling along with dog in tow, dancing on a tabletop at Ninochka's Bar – the effect is irrevocable. 'And as they marched by, these feet seemed capable of achieving miracles – of wiping out centuries in an hour – because they were free.'

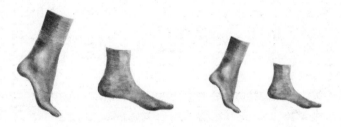

Another survivor of the Holocaust was that intellectual wanderer George Steiner. All but two of his Jewish classmates in his Paris *lycée* were to perish in Auschwitz, like Helga's father, but Steiner grew up to become, as Amos Oz told me in Tel Aviv, 'one of the great cultural middlemen and readers of the twentieth century. He makes books pass from culture to culture.'

One rainy May day in his eighty-seventh year, Steiner accepted my request to go on a walk with him.

Even though he was then nearing the end of his life, George Steiner continued to outpace most of his generation. Every sentence he spoke was a sprint in a marathon. With a conjurer's flourish, he produced a visitor's card for me. On it, a message scrawled in black ink, and a date: '3. 4. 1921'.

'Read who sent it!'

An italicised name explained the excitement: *Prof Dr. Freud*.

The handwritten message was from Sigmund Freud to Steiner's father, Frederick, 'an austere, difficult man' who worked for a bank in Vienna. Freud and Frederick Steiner were friends. They'd walk in Vienna, in the hills around, and talk together. Steiner's connective mind found it impossible to imagine that Adolf Hitler, Freud, Steiner's father, and also Gustav Mahler, did not pass each other on the Ringstrasse walking. 'It's inescapable. They are there, in the same city, for two or three years.'

My short walk with George Steiner on that drizzly afternoon took us from his book-lined drawing room in Cambridge, out to his purpose-built study at the end of the garden, and back. A journey of less than a hundred yards. Yet, I like to think it was an illustration of Jorge Luis Borges's celebrated parable: of the old wanderer who draws a map of everywhere he has been in his life, and discovers that he has delineated his own face.

Steiner's first walks were in Paris. Rue Lafontaine, Place Victor Hugo. 'In summer as a child I would go to our retreat in Normandy where Monet painted, Étretat.' Later, based in Geneva, he discovered mountain-climbing, and scaled the rock face of the Salève, as Borges had done, in the days when he could see ('I've never met a person who seemed to need eyelids less').

'What's your favourite walk?'

'In the Jura, near where Courbet had a house, a group of hills above Ornans; a wonderful landscape combining ancient reminders of civilisation with wild country – bits of Roman and Gallic fortifications and very exciting traces of the Burgundian wars.'

At the time of our stroll, Steiner had just reissued *The Idea of Europe*, in which he had written about the importance of walking. Kant's chronometrically precise traverse of Königsberg. The rambles of Kierkegaard through Copenhagen. The portly Coleridge routinely covering thirty miles per diem across difficult, mountainous ground, composing poetry or intricate theological arguments as he strode. It was something that differentiated us from America, Steiner believed. 'One does not go on foot from one American town to the next.' Europe, by contrast, had been moulded and humanised by human feet. It wasn't too much to say that our entire philosophy had been conditioned by walking, by the simple action of putting one foot before another.

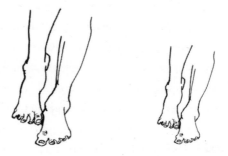

My grandfather was a tremendous walker. 'In all walks,' went one of his rules, 'one should imitate Lot's wife once every five minutes at least' – and look backwards.

His name was S. P. B. Mais. If I glance back at him, I see a hyperactive author of over two hundred travel books – the vast majority describing his journeys made slowly and on foot from one English town to the next – who rose to prominence during the Depression, when he became known as the 'Ambassador of the English Countryside'. In January 1932, the BBC commissioned a topographical series, *This Unknown Island*, to encourage tourism to Britain's holiday resorts. 'SPB' (as he was popularly known) travelled to seventeen regions. His message for people to get out and explore what lay on their doorsteps, preferably in walking boots, held a powerful appeal to those who could not afford the cost of travelling abroad, still less a car. The public responded in huge numbers. In July 1932, he was joined by 16,000 people on the Sussex Downs to watch the sun rise over the Iron Age fort at Chanctonbury Ring. Four special trains had to be laid on for this midnight excursion. But my grandmother's favourite story was the occasion when SPB was invited to give a talk at Lewes Prison. He became so excited and enthusiastic about the English countryside – 'no country in the world can hold a candle to England so far as beauty of landscape is concerned' – that he found himself urging the inmates to get out more, to see more of it for themselves.

It was SPB's imperishable conviction that 'there is as much technique in walking as there is in singing or writing' (*Listen to the Country, 1939*). Another of his rules: 'Never cover more than a mile an hour.' It was essential, he maintained, to dawdle. 'To see England aright you have to acquire the sauntering habit, to find time to lean over gates and look at the crops, to sit on bridges and watch the water flow by.' Perhaps his biggest rule was to travel alone. 'I have always been a strong advocate of walking by oneself.' He was critical of walking clubs and ramblers, who travelled to be social, their fiercest anxiety about tea.

The very fact of having a companion keeps their minds on a workaday plane. If they were by themselves they would stand a chance of really being taken out of themselves, of hearing, of seeing, of smelling, of touching, of communing with

themselves and being still … Only when we are alone can we
hear the songs of birds, the hum of insects, the whole invisible
choir around us.

For my manic, probably bipolar grandfather, as for C. P. Cavafy,
the journey on foot and not the destination was the thing. 'It's
not the getting to places that matters on a walk, it's the walk
itself,' he wrote in *Weekends in England* (1933). 'I go into the
country alone, exactly as an empty pitcher goes to the well – to
be filled.'

My grandfather was never one to obey his own rules. In periods of turmoil and stress, of which there were many, he pulled
on his 'thorn-proof knickerbockers' and walked over the Sussex
Downs with the young naturalist Henry Williamson, later the
author of *Tarka the Otter*. 'On these smooth slopes all tangles
seem to come unravelled, and all problems solved.' Just like
Paddy Leigh Fermor and Bruce Chatwin when they strode
together, chatting, through the Peloponnesian landscape, SPB
was struggling, whether consciously or not, to enact Diogenes'
formula *solvitur ambulando* ('it is solved by walking'). When
using strenuous exercise to self-medicate, he often invoked
G. M. Trevelyan's adage: 'I have two doctors, my left leg and my
right.'

Yet sometimes, in the company of Williamson, my grandfather didn't dawdle at one mile an hour, so much as shoot off like
an unleashed dog. His companion recalled him striding vacantly
ahead at a furious rate, manifestly *not* looking backwards, 'and
though it almost exhausted him, he breathed, when I was near
him, I noticed, almost silently through his open mouth. He
seemed to be walking to escape his thoughts: a horsefly had got
into his brain.'

On at least two occasions, SPB claimed to have walked through the night.

*   *   *

It's a whole other experience walking in the dark. To start with, it sounds different. A lion roars in the early morning because the noise carries that much more in the damp. At night, the sound of tyres on the road is muffled, as if absorbed by the darkness, and I need a torch to ward off the Ocado delivery van when, with no warning, it roars up our country lane in Wiltshire.

Taking Sancho for his last walk of the day, I am dragged at the dog's forceful pace into a black and white negative of my ante-meridian world. Lights on in houses that are lived in. The flashes of burglar alarms and big-screen TVs. I see other walkers out, with blinking miners' lights and wearing high-vis jackets. Walkers without torches, or unoccupied houses with window-panes like empty eye sockets, become menacing.

Then the visibility factor. Ahead of me in the night some-where, his golden contours lapped at and diminished by the winter gloom, Sancho takes on a spectral glimmer that reminds me not so much of the fast-receding shape of my grandfather in one of his tearaway moods but a glow-worm. Glow-worms have died out in most places in England, surviving only on unim-proved land. Patrolling this way and that at the end of his lead, Sancho sees me, but I frequently have no inkling where he is. He keeps disappearing, swallowed by the dark, and then reappear-ing, like that small yellowish pulse of light I glimpsed one midnight on a disused railway track in Cumbria. He has no competition from overhead. This is Wiltshire in December 2020, there are no stars.

Last, the temperature. 'All true walkers prefer walking in winter,' believed my grandfather in *The Happiest Days of My Life* (1953), the second of his three autobiographies. 'In the winter we walk to keep fit, to get warm, to enjoy the keen cold air, which threatens to kill us if we loiter, but is a tonic if we keep moving.'

Clearly, I am not my grandfather's grandson. In any other year, I wouldn't be here in this freezing black Wiltshire lane, trying to keep pace with a semi-invisible dog during lockdown. I would be on the other side of the world, in Tasmania, looking up at the Milky Way, in starlight that is almost bright enough to read by.

There's a dirt road in Tasmania which winds through a forested landscape planted with tall and ancient eucalypts, where it's possible to believe that no one has put foot. In 2007, I drove along this road with my father in the sole vehicle to be kicking up dust that day, maybe that month. Some miles on, we passed a signpost pointing right into the bush to our right and bearing the name Synotts Road – and we both had the same reaction. In our combined travels, neither of us could have imagined living in so remote a place.

'If you buried yourself away down there,' said my father, peering as far as he could up the reddish track, 'no one would find you.'

Extraordinarily, the owner of this imagined paradise turned out to be someone we knew. Every year since, Geoff Bull, a winemaker whose children attended the same local school as mine, has invited our family to his property at the end of that tributary. Over the last thirteen years, two or three other families have always joined in the ritual.

We camp out for the night in tents around a fire, and usually don't stop talking until after midnight, while the flames warm our faces, playing over them, as if to read their cartography and to discover what extra lines the months have added to our features since we last met.

Then when everyone is asleep, I unzip my tent and go for a walk.

On my very first 'Synotts', as we now commonly call this annual get-together – '"St Anthony" spelled backwards? No one knows the significance. If you find out, we'd be very impressed,' says Geoff – I stepped out beneath a pair of colossal bluegums into a large level clearing the size of a cricket field. It was two in the morning. The air was abnormally still and silent, and overhead the autumn darkness was pricked with more stars than I was conscious of having seen in a sky. The starlight fell on strange white objects. In a sort of trance, I bent down to touch the bones of kangaroos and sheep – but their presence on the ground was most unusual. In any previous year, these bones would have been hoovered up during the night by Tasmanian devils.

The devil – the world's largest carnivorous marsupial – is to be found only in Tasmania. The size of a black and white pug dog, it has a powerful jaw that makes it an efficient nocturnal scavenger, and takes its diabolical name from a piercing howl that has been likened to an exhaust pipe dragging on bitumen. But a mysterious cancer had decimated Tasmania's devil population, casting a hush on the bush. Virtually overnight, ever since the appearance of this 'devil facial tumour disease', the species is facing extinction in the way of its larger marsupial cousin, the Tasmanian tiger; not to forget the island's original inhabitants, the Tasmanian Aborigines. It's in the middle of one of their traditional hunting grounds, it turns out, that I have pitched my tent.

Much of what little is known about Tasmania's Aborigines we owe to a prickly nineteenth-century English missionary, George Augustus Robinson, who spent lengthy periods travelling with the tribes through the bush, and writing down their customs and beliefs.

Two of his entries have relevance for nocturnal walkers.

On 13 June 1831, Robinson tilted his diary towards the firelight and pencilled the following observation: 'The aborigines of Van Diemen's Land [as Tasmania then was known] are noctivagant, i.e. they walk at night.'

Not only that, but the Aborigines believed in a devil, Raegowrapper, who, if you went walking out in the bush on your own at night, would be responsible for you not coming back.

Tellingly, Raegowrapper was most active during those years which saw deadly infections or viruses. According to Robinson, Raegowrapper (pronounced 'radje-eeoo-wrapper') lived in the darkness and infected you with a 'distemper', rendering you a corpse. 'The natives have a tradition,' Robinson wrote, 'that when one of the tribe dies of this infection, he walks by night, having a quantity of the distemper in a kangaroo skin, and imparts it to the rest of the tribe.' Their longstanding belief in this tradition suggests that the Tasmanian Aborigines would have fitted our plague year of 2020 into a narrative much less disruptive and more universally accepted than we appear capable of achieving: to them, the coronavirus would have been merely another manifestation of, say, the 'distemper' that from time to time ran through not only the Aboriginal but the Tasmanian tiger population.

But back to that first Synotts. As I thought scattered thoughts on devils, and picked my way between unscavenged kangaroo bones, all of a sudden an army of dense, black shadows reared up before me.

My heart beat faster than a voodoo drum. On this silent night in the bush, the imagination invested those shadows with intense significance, as the noctivagant spirits of the vanished Oyster Bay Tribe. In an instinctive gesture, I kneeled – also to check their outline against the Milky Way … which was when I saw that they weren't dead warriors levelling *ti*-tree spears at me, but tussocks of marram grass.

*　　*　　*

Not long after that first Synotts, a man my age came to the door of our beach house on Tasmania's east coast and introduced himself as its previous owner.

To my amazement and joy, Brad Wilson told me that where the house now stands was once an observatory. Brad had erected it from corrugated iron on a frame of pine trees that he'd chopped down himself, and on the top of this he had fitted a slide-off roof that opened to the sky. Inside, he had pinned up star charts and installed a car battery to operate a ten-inch Newtonian telescope.

'The big reason I came here,' Brad said, 'was for this wonderful southern sky.'

The main action was the Milky Way of which we were a part, but Brad also saw the Aurora Australis flaring up from the southern horizon in sheets of red and green. He counted innumerable galaxies, including, he said, the Virgo Cluster – 'that would be 2,000 galaxies, all in a small area as large as you can make with your thumb and index finger'. Not once in those years had Brad seen a UFO – as a sizeable number claim to have spied in these southern parts – but one night he witnessed a *bolis*, a huge shooting star that lit the entire sky and left a smoke trail that he observed for a full two minutes through his telescope. 'And one night,' he said, 'I'm on a night walk, I come back here, walking back through the pines, and something is glowing on the ground, not a torch as I'd thought, but a patch of mushrooms, glowing like you'd never believe.'

When you walk at night, you view the world as the blind Borges saw it. (As a teenager in Buenos Aires, I once walked with Borges for some blocks through his sprawling, noisy, decadent city. 'Yellow, I can make out, like that ...' and he stopped to unlink arms and touch a gold-painted placard. 'Everything else seems an indistinct haze.')

You have thoughts that you don't have during the day. It's not merely shapes on the ground that ignite the imagination in a different way, but those in the heavens above. More so than in the overly clouded (and polluted) northern hemisphere, something about the southern sky – in particular the bright scarf of the Milky Way – confirms that we are indeed no bigger than the ubiquitous grain of sand, of which Tasmania's deserted beaches contain billions.

A few nights after Brad's visit, with the full moon rising over the Freycinet Peninsula, I coerced my seven-year-old son to walk with me down to the beach. He kicked and screamed about going into the dark – but the moonlight calmed him, and all at once his stringy figure loped past.

It's a rare beach where you can walk into sunrise, and at the end of the day into sunset. Officially, this spit of white sand, stretching east to west, is named Bagehot Point after an early military commander of the local town. Over the past two hundred years, it's also been known as The Isthmus, The Spit, The Peninsula, Sandy Point, Meredith's Sandbank, Scrubby Point – and now Dolphin Sands. To the natives of the Oyster Bay Tribe, it was – if you'll forgive the translation (although, heartbreakingly, no one has survived who might contest it) – Larwey Niree Tana Bona, Pathway to the Gods. You were obliged once in your life to walk along it, on a pilgrimage to the arresting peninsula in front of us, where a family of Aboriginal deities were believed to sleep; and over the granite peaks of which, their dense colour smoky and compact like a watercolour pigment, the sun would in a few hours rise.

The night sky was so bright it had turned blue. The sandy path was pitted with hard-edged shadows that I'd never noticed in sunlight, more reminiscent of the surface of the moon. In the bush, there was masses of activity. Aside from the absent devils, all the macropods were out foraging; the wrens and honeyeaters were singing as if it was day; and along Dolphin Sands the scrolling waves glimmered with phosphorescence.

There'd been a storm a few days before, but now the bay was calm. The moon glinted through a film of sea mist, and overhead I was able to make out Saturn and Orion's Belt and the Southern Cross. I walked on, the bare soles of my feet making squeaking noises on the fine sand. I could have been walking on a beach composed of stars. A mystical experience, broken by a small voice:

'Dad, I'm cold,' and he started racing back.

'Careful of snakes!' I called, looking round.

But all I heard were his feet thumping the path with a sound like a heavy fruit dropping.

The Returns Home

Patrick Gale

Walking is in my blood and as much a part of my daily routine as drinking flat whites and visiting the greenhouse to check on seedlings. Writers are notoriously sedentary and prone to poor health. I'm no exception in the ease with which I start living so much in my head, as a book develops, that I forget to live in my body. Having dogs helps. Hounds are not emotionally needy dogs when walking; whippets and greyhounds have none of the collie's need for constant affirmative interaction with its human but seem quite content to trot independently from smell to fascinating smell, occasionally breaking off to send up a pheasant or make a show of chasing a rabbit. They enjoy walks hugely but they're not forever nudging you to say, 'I'm enjoying my walk. I am. Are you? Are you enjoying yours? Are you really?' They are not like Dalmatians and don't require miles a day, but they still need two good outings and that fits neatly into my routine. So on a good day I'll walk them before I start work and I walk them again when I break off before it gets dark.

Friends who know the country have described how Russian houses have an unheated porch or outer chamber, unheated but not as dangerously cold as outside, so that visitors in winter can pause there to cool down or warm up before moving into the heated interior or bitter outdoors. These daily walks of mine are the writer's equivalent; they provide a mental chamber where I shake off domestic concerns like so many snowy outer garments – the malfunctioning switch in the airing cupboard, the difficulty of ridding the house of plastic – to re-enter the novel I'm working on. It works in the other direction too, the evening walk letting me process the day's writing in my head, depressurise and become normal again. Often the day's writing will have been frustrating or ragged, or will only finally have taken off just as the garden is shading over and the relentlessly punctual whippet slides sharp little paws onto my thigh. On evenings like that the day's second walk turns into an inkless continuation of the task in hand and I'll find that, while walking, I can easily reorder the material and see the way ahead as I could not when glaring down at my notebook and doodling in its margins.

It's not that I don't enjoy these routine walks or take them in – I am quietly obsessed by wildflowers and birds and carry a mental catalogue of the ones I'm likely to spot – but these are not walks to go anywhere specific or to seek out something in particular. The dogs and I have a short repertoire of routes around our farm. There are purely field-based walks, particularly pleasing in the weeks after our harvesting of barley has reopened large stretches of land or when, as at this moment, in June, there are adjacent fields that won't be ploughed up until later in the summer, so that skylarks nest in them, goldfinches charm, and an abundance of wild flowers turns a couple of acres into a second garden. Some field-based routes have magnificent sea views out beyond the Longships to the Scillies, others are better for bad weather, taking in a sheltering valley.

Then there is the route we call 'round the block' which crosses one length of the farm's horseshoe shape, joins a dramatic stretch of cliffside coast path then re-enters the farm from the horseshoe's other branch. This is much the best route for thinking on because it requires only one choice – do we go anticlockwise and have a fierce cliff climb at the end, or clockwise and have a sharp descent and a steadier climb back up? This is the route where, despite seals, choughs, dizzying colonies of flowers on the cliff edge and *Rebecca* title-sequence breakers on the rocks, I most often find I have walked a mile or two and taken in nothing beyond the fact that I have been deep in thought. I will occasionally come up for air, as it were, obliged to, perhaps, by meeting someone coming the other way or (maddeningly) overlapping with someone walking in the same direction; but even when I do, the daily familiarity of what I'm admiring afresh, be it coronets of wild carrot or a kestrel quivering on the air above a mouse, somehow fails to nudge my thoughts aside as something brand new might.

There's an especially meditative quality to the seaward walks because, for most of their length, there are no houses in view; the climb up across our fields from the coast path is steady and it's only on the brow of the climb that, all at once, church tower and village are revealed again, a cue to put aside thoughts of characters and plot and be again a member of a household.

*   *   *

We were a walking family. My mother was especially energetic and restless, and keen that we should always be out and seeing. Holidays ushered in a rich programme of improving excursions but even in term time there were weekly walks. There must have been weeks when torrential rain or the demands of her beloved gardens kept us home, but my memory of boyhood Sundays is that there was always a longish walk in the afternoon followed by tea. And that long after we had one by one stopped going with our parents to church (a place to which my mother had been known to lure us with the promise of a sugary bun from a Sunday baker on the way home), we walked as a family. On downs, on disused train lines (under the influence of my steam-mad brothers), up to Iron Age forts and up, up to fly kites on some old drovers' road or pilgrimage route, we walked. Between them, our parents were as good as Observer's Books made flesh; he identified the periods of church building and breeds of cattle, she named wild flowers and trees. So family walks were as talkative and instructional as school. They were also tiring, as I was the youngest, fattest and by some way the last to grow the family long legs, so I was often to be found dramatically wailing, far behind their striding silhouettes, crying, 'Wait for me!' At some point, however, I realised that the real magic lay in that falling back, escaping the naming of mushrooms and quizzing on the difference between barley and wheat, and escaping into my thoughts, even as my fat little legs stomped on in the wake of the striding grown-ups.

*   *   *

The returns home from childhood walks have conflated in my memory into one deeply comforting array of steaming tea, hot buttered toast and cake. There is talk, constant talk, and the unambiguous smell of recently dried-off dog. There must have

been summer equivalents – lemonade and cake in the garden, perhaps – but it's the winter returns that cast the most powerful spell. I conjure them up now when I return from my second walk of the day, a walk where all the talk has been in my head. The sun is setting over the sea behind me, making my shadow and those of the dogs and our cattle crazily long. Lights are coming on in the distant village, around the church and the campsite.

I will rub down and feed the dogs now, put on the kettle, and re-enter the world.

Biographies

Duncan Minshull was a producer at BBC Radio and now freelances in audio production. He also publishes books about walking, and titles include *While Wandering*, *Beneath My Feet*, and *Sauntering: Writers Walk Europe*. He has written about walking for *The Times*, the *Financial Times*, the *Guardian*, *Condé Nast Traveller*, *Vogue*, *Psychologies*, *Slightly Foxed*, the *Big Issue* and the *Lady*. He lives in west London.

Richard Ford is an American novelist, story writer and essayist. His work has been translated into thirty-five languages and has won many American and international prizes, including the Princess of Asturias Prize in Spain, the Prix Femina in France, and the La Lettura Prize in Italy, as well as the Pulitzer and Library of Congress Prizes for fiction in his own country. He lives in Boothbay, Maine, with his wife, Kristina Ford.

Tim Parks is a novelist, essayist and translator based in Milan. He is author of eighteen novels, including *Europa*, *Destiny* and *In Extremis*. His many non-fiction works include *Italian Neighbours*, *A Season with Verona* and *Italian Life*, as well as a memoir on chronic pain and meditation, *Teach Us to Sit Still*. His latest book is *The Hero's Way*, which follows in the footsteps of Giuseppe Garibaldi.

Ingrid Persaud was born in Trinidad. Her debut novel, *Love After Love*, won the Costa First Novel Award 2020. She also won the BBC National Short Story Award in 2018 and the Commonwealth Short Story Prize in 2017. She read law at the LSE and was an academic before studying fine art at Goldsmiths and Central Saint Martins. Her writing has appeared in several newspapers and magazines including *Granta*, *Prospect*, *Five Dials*, *Alexander*, the *Guardian* and *National Geographic*.

A. L. Kennedy was born in Dundee and lived for almost thirty years in Glasgow. She is the author of eight literary novels, one fable, one YA novel, seven collections of short stories, three books of non-fiction. She also writes for film, television, theatre and radio. She has been granted numerous awards in five countries, including the Costa Prize and the Heinrich Heine Prize.

Pico Iyer is the author of fifteen books, translated into twenty-three languages. Recent works are twinned books on his long-time home near Nara in Japan, *Autumn Light* and *A Beginner's Guide to Japan*.

Keshava Guha is the author of the novel *Accidental Magic* (HarperCollins, 2019). Raised in Bangalore and educated in the US, he has lived for many years in Delhi. His journalism – on politics, culture and sport – has appeared in a range of Indian and international publications.

Jessica J. Lee is a British-Canadian-Taiwanese writer and environmental historian, and winner of the 2020 Hilary Weston Writers' Trust Prize for Nonfiction, the 2020 Boardman Tasker Award for Mountain Literature and the 2019 RBC Taylor Emerging Writer Award. She is the author of two books of nature writing: *Turning* (2017) and *Two Trees Make a Forest* (2019). Jessica is the founding editor of the *Willowherb Review* and a researcher at the University of Cambridge. She lives in London.

Sally Bayley's books include *The Private Life of the Diary*, the best-selling memoir *Girl with Dove*, and its recent sequel, *No Boys Play Here*. In 1990, she was the first child to go to university from West Sussex County Council Care services and studied at St Andrews University. She is currently a Lecturer in English at Hertford College, Oxford, and also teaches on the Sarah Lawrence visiting programme at Wadham College, Oxford.

Harland Miller is a writer and artist. Born in Yorkshire, he studied at Chelsea School of Art, graduating in 1988 with an MA. He published his first novel, *Slow Down Arthur, Stick to Thirty*, to critical acclaim in 2000, and has also written for various newspapers and magazines and for BBC Radio. He is currently working on his memoir, *One Bar Electric Memoir*.

Will Self is the author of twenty-five books, some of which have been translated into twenty-five languages. His most recent book was the memoir *Will*. He lives in south London, and holds the Chair in Contemporary Thought at Brunel University. A regular broadcaster and a prolific journalist, Self is well known as a commentator on issues affecting the built environment, and a writer concerned with places, spaces, and what lies between them.

Irenosen Okojie was born in Nigeria and moved to England as a child. Her debut novel, *Butterfly Fish* (2015), won a Betty Trask Award and her first story collection, *Speak Gigantular* (2016), was shortlisted for the inaugural Jhalak Prize, a Shirley Jackson Award and the 2017 Edge Hill Short Story Prize. *Nudibranch* (2019) was longlisted for the Jhalak Prize, with her story 'Grace Jones' winning the AKO Caine Prize for African Writing. Her novel *Curandera* will be published by Dialogue Books in 2022. She is a Fellow of the Royal Society of Literature.

Joanna Kavenna grew up in Britain, and has also lived in the USA, France, Germany, China, Sri Lanka and Scandinavia. She is the author of several works of fiction, non-fiction and much that is both, including *A Field Guide to Reality*, *The Ice Museum*, *Inglorious* and *Zed*. She was named as one of *Granta*'s Best of Young British Novelists in 2013.

Agnès Poirier is a journalist and writer who lives between Paris and London. She is the author of *Left Bank: Art, Passion and the Rebirth of Paris, 1940–1950* and *Notre-Dame: The Soul of France*.

Sinéad Gleeson's debut essay collection, *Constellations*, won Non-Fiction Book of the Year at the 2019 Irish Book Awards and the Dalkey Literary Award. She has edited four short-story anthologies and is co-editor with Kim Gordon of *This Woman's Work: Essays on Music* (2022). She is currently working on a novel.

Kathleen Rooney is a founding editor of Rose Metal Press, as well as a founding member of Poems While You Wait. Her most recent books include the novel *Lillian Boxfish Takes a Walk* and *The Listening Room: A Novel of Georgette and Loulou Magritte*. Her World War I novel *Cher Ami and Major Whittlesey* was published by Penguin in August 2020, and her criticism appears in the *New York Times Magazine*, the Poetry Foundation website, the *Chicago Tribune*, the *Los Angeles Review of Books* and elsewhere. She lives in Chicago and teaches at DePaul University.

Josephine Rowe is an Australian author of three short-story collections and a novel, *A Loving, Faithful Animal*. She holds fellowships from the Wallace Stegner Program at Stanford University, the International Writing Program at the University of Iowa, the BR Whiting Studio in Rome, and is currently the Janice B. and Milford D. Gerton/Arts and Letters Foundation Fellow at the New York Public Library. Her most recent story collection is *Here Until August*.

Kamila Shamsie is the author of seven novels, which have been translated into over thirty languages. Her most recent novel, *Home Fire*, won the Women's Prize for Fiction, was shortlisted for the Costa Novel Award and longlisted for the Man Booker Prize. A Vice-President and Fellow of the Royal Society of Literature, and one of *Granta*'s Best of Young British Novelists, she grew up in Karachi, and now lives in London.

Cynan Jones was born on the west coast of Wales in 1975. His fiction is published in twenty or so countries and has won numerous awards. He has also written for television and radio, and his short stories have appeared in a wide range of publications including *Granta* and the *New Yorker*.

Nicholas Shakespeare is a novelist and biographer who has been translated into twenty-two languages. His books include *The Dancer Upstairs*, which was turned into a film by John Malkovich, and the authorised biography of Bruce Chatwin. He is currently researching a new life of Ian Fleming. He divides his time between Wiltshire and Tasmania.

Patrick Gale is the author of numerous novels, including *Rough Music*, *Notes from an Exhibition* and *A Place Called Winter*, and of the BBC screenplay *Man in an Orange Shirt*. His most recent novel is *Mother's Boy*. He lives on the most westerly farm in England with his husband, the sculptor and farmer Aidan Hicks.

Acknowledgements

The stories in *Where My Feet Fall* attest to the fact that walking is both a lone and a group thing, set off how you will. Putting these pages together always meant moving with others, and my initial thanks go to the 'cavalcade' at William Collins. To Arabella Pike who immediately liked the idea and said something like 'yes, forward!' To Jo Thompson who was a great help with commissioning everyone. To Katy Archer as the indispensable project editor. To Kit Shepherd and Jane Donovan for diligent copyediting and proofreading. To Graham Holmes for making the book look so good. To Jessica Barnfield for the audio version. And to Helen Ellis for matters of publicity and promotion.

To the writers themselves – thank you for walking in trying times or for reimagining old walks; and for providing the accompanying images, which show you are skilled sketchers, mappers and snappers. Thanks also to Arizona Smith and Blythe Kavenna, Gillian Johnson and Angela Minshull, who visualised with style for Sally Bayley, Joanna Kavenna, Nicholas Shakespeare and Sinéad Gleeson respectively.

I reckoned a stroll around my neighbourhood of Maida Vale in west London would spark off ideas on how to headline the collection, but after a fair few turns ... no, nothing came to light. So a final nod to Jessica J. Lee, from whose piece I lifted the title, and she was fine about it.

DM.